# CONQUERING IN CHRIST
A Brief Commentary and Study Guide
On the Book of Revelation

By:
Dr. Ian A. Fair

**HCU Media LLC**
Accra, Ghana · Frisco, TX

# CONQUERING IN CHRIST
A Brief Commentary and Study Guide on the Book of Revelation

**HCU Media LLC**
www.HCUMedia.com

First Published and Copyright © 2010
By Dr. Ian A. Fair & the Center for Church Resources
www.centercr.com

Published and Copyright © 2012
By Dr. Ian A. Fair & HCU Media LLC

ISBN-13: 978-1-939468-00-0 (US Paperback Edition)

Also available in electronic book form and International Editions – for more information reference our website: www.HCUMedia.com

Additional Resources available at www.HCUMedia.com/conquering

Printed in the USA

ALL RIGHTS RESERVED
No part of this publication may be reproduced, stored in a retrieval system, or transmitted in any form by any means – electronic, mechanical, photocopying, recording or otherwise – without prior written consent.

Scripture quotations, unless otherwise noted, are from The Holy Bible, Revised Standard Version, copyright 1971, Zondervan Bible Publishers.

Cover Design by Dale Henry – www.dalehenrydesign.com

First Edition December 2012
10 9 8 7 6 5 4 3 2 1

# CONTENTS

Preface .................................................................... 9

Important Scriptures ................................................ 11

Selected Bibliography ............................................. 13

Chapter 1: An Introduction to the story: What is Revelation All About? ............................................................ 15

Chapter 2: The Strange Language and Style of Revelation, and the Message of Revelation ........................... 23

Chapter 3: Introduction to the Theology and Relevant Lessons of Revelation ......................................... 35

Chapter 4: The Prologue of Revelation: Revelation Chapter 1 ............................................ 43

Chapter 5: The Seven Letters to the Seven Churches: Revelation Chapters 2 & 3 .................................. 51

Chapter 6: The Throne Room and Scroll: Revelation 4; 5:1-8:5 ......................................... 61

Chapter 7: The Seven Warning Trumpets: Revelation 8 & 9 ................................................. 73

Chapter 8: The Second Interlude and Seventh Trumpet: Revelation 10 & 11 ............................................ 79

Chapter 9: The Christ and Victory – The Climax of Revelation: Revelation 12 ...................................... 87

Chapter 10: The Two Beasts and the Lamb: Revelation 13 & 14 ............................................ 95

Chapter 11: God's Judgment on Rome Consummated: Revelation 15-19 ................................................ 103

Chapter 12: The 1000 Year Binding of Satan and the Reign of the Martyrs Revelation 20:1-20:15 ................ 113

Chapter 13: The Finale: Revelation 21:1-22:21 ................. 121

Addendum I: Lessons for Today from Revelation and
    Millennial Views ................................................ 133
Addendum II: The Chiastic Structure of Revelation .......... 147
Addendum III: The Story of Revelation ............................ 149
Glossary of Terms ............................................................ 153

# Preface

This brief commentary is intended to serve as a guide for those teaching Revelation in a Bible class or as a guide for personal study.

Over the years I have taught small group classes, congregational Bible classes, and university classes and have felt the need for a short commentary that bridges between some basic studies and the more scholarly and detailed commentaries. I have written this little work with an eye on the reader who does not want to get bogged down in academic details and yet who wants something with meaning to it. I have tried to stay in contact with the latest research and publications in the field of Revelation. The bibliography below will reference some of the more advanced studies.

I am indebted to my family and friends who have through the years encouraged me to write a comprehensive commentary. Finally, *Conquering With Christ,* the result of 40 years researching and teaching in the field of Revelation and apocalyptic eschatology was published through ACU Press in 2012. My wife June and sons Deon, Nigel, and Douglas, and their wives Susan, Joy, and Sherri have added their voices of support and encouragement through the years. So I dedicate this little work to my family.

However, I also owe much to a host of university and college students over the past 40 years who have patiently listened to my teaching. They have added their insightful questions and comments to my research and teaching. This work would not have reached this point without them.

Finally, this work is offered with the prayer that it will encourage Christians and others to realize the triumphant victory we have in Christ over Satan and his forces of evil that challenge us on every front of our lives. My prayer is that it will offer hope to those who struggle under the pressures of life, and ultimately bring glory to God our Father and his Son, Jesus Christ.

In the word of our Jewish friends and ancestors in Christ, "We praise the Holy One, Blessed be He!" To this Rabbi Akiba added "A man should always accustom himself to say 'Whatever the All-merciful does, He does for the best.'" (Abraham Cohen, *Everyman's Talmud*, BN Publishing, 2008.)

Our God is a Righteous God! To Him be all the glory!

# Important Scriptures

### Rev 1:1-3

*The revelation of Jesus Christ, which God gave him to show to his servants what must soon take place; and he made it known by sending his angel to his servant John, $^2$ who bore witness to the word of God and to the testimony of Jesus Christ, even to all that he saw. $^3$ Blessed is he who reads aloud the words of the prophecy, and blessed are those who hear, and who keep what is written therein; for the time is near.*

### Rev 12:10, 11

*And I heard a loud voice in heaven, saying, "Now the salvation and the power and the kingdom of our God and the authority of his Christ have come, for the accuser of our brethren has been thrown down, who accuses them day and night before our God. And they have conquered him by the blood of the Lamb and by the word of their testimony, for they loved not their lives even unto death.*

### Rom 8:37-39

*No, in all these things we are more than conquerors through him who loved us. $^{38}$ For I am sure that neither death, nor life, nor angels, nor principalities, nor things present, nor things to come, nor powers, $^{39}$ nor height, nor depth, nor anything else in all creation, will be able to separate us from the love of God in Christ Jesus our Lord*

# CONQUERING IN CHRIST

### A COMMENTARY ON THE BOOK OF REVELATION

This study is a brief introductory commentary on the Book of Revelation plus an Addendum on Millennial Studies and a brief Glossary of relevant terms.

The intention of this commentary is to serve as a teaching or study guide for Bible Classes and Personal Study

## Selected Bibliography

The following is a useful bibliography to this study:
Aune, David. *Revelation*, Word Books, 1997, (3 vols, an advanced commentary with extended bibliography).
Bass, Clarence B. *Backgrounds to Dispensationalism*, Wipf & Stock Publishers, 1960.
Bauckham, Richard, *The Theology of the Book of Revelation*, Cambridge University Press, 1993.
Richard Bauckham, *The Climax of Prophecy: Studies in the Book of Revelation*, T & T Clark, 1993.
Beale, G. K. *The Book of Revelation*, Wm. B. Eerdmans, 1999.
Beasley-Murray, G. R. *Revelation*, Wm. B. Eerdmans, 1974, 1981.
Boring, M. Eugene. *Revelation*, John Knox Press, 1989.
Caird, G. B. *The Revelation of St. John*, Harper and Row, 1966.
Eusebius, *Ecclesiastical History*, vol. 1, Loeb Classical Library, 1965.
Fair, Ian A. *Revelation*, Hillcrest Publishers, ACU Press, 1998.
Fair, Ian A. *Conquering With Christ*, ACU Press, 2012.
Freedman, David Noel, Ed., *The Anchor Bible Dictionary*, 1992.

Frend, W. H. C. *Martyrdom and Persecution on the Early Church*, Basil Blackwell, 1965, Reprinted by Baker Book House, 1982.

Hemer, Colin J. *The Letters to the Seven Churches of Asia in Their Local Setting*, Sheffield Academic Press, 1986.

Humble, Bill & Ian A. Fair, *The Seven Churches of Asia*, Gospel Advocate, 1995.

Mounce, Robert H. *The Book of Revelation*, Wm. B. Eerdmans, 1977.

Nickelsburg, George W. E. *Jewish Literature Between the Bible and the Mishna*, Fortress, 2005.

Osborne, Grant. *Revelation*, Baker Academics, 2002.

Vanderkam, James C. *The Dead Sea Scrolls Today*, Eerdmans, 1994.

# Chapter 1

# An Introduction to the story: What is Revelation All About?

## Introduction

When the subject of Revelation crops up in many discussions a variety of ideas spring to mind! Some immediately think of the *Left Behind* series of books by Tim Lahaye which play on the concept of a supposed Rapture in which those who do not belong to Christ are left behind as the faithful are taken up into the air to meet Jesus when he returns. Careful study will reveal that that is not the message of Revelation. Neither is it an accurate study of 1 Thess 4:13 following! Others immediately conclude that the book of Revelation is about the end of the world and the final judgment. Certainly the book of Revelation does involve some features surrounding the end of the World. In this regard some read into Revelation a message relating to the "signs of the times". In fact when we merely think of Revelation several confusing millennial possibilities are offered. In this study I plan to ask John what he had in mind when God through Jesus instructed him to write this magnificent, challenging, and exciting book.

In this first chapter I plan to introduce you to the book of Revelation and its wonderful message.

Revelation is perhaps the most exciting and positive book in the Bible! You can summarize the theology of Revelation in two words (I want you to memorize them and stamp them indelibly in your mind. They are *Victory* and *Conquering*! Hence the title of this commentary, *Conquering in Christ*.

We will learn in this study that one Greek word for *victory* is *sotēria*, the same word which is translated in some contexts as *salvation*!

We will also learn that a prominent Greek word found seven times in Rev 2 and 3 is *nikaō* which is translated in the Revised

Standard Version of Revelation as *conquering*. It is translated in the NIV as *overcoming*. We will learn that overcoming is not the most felicitous translation even though it is a possible meaning of the word *nikaō*.

With this in mind read Rom 8:35ff and Rev 12:10ff. They are both vital to our understanding of the theology of Revelation. Notice that Rom 8:35ff speaks of being *more than conquerors* in Christ. This so impressed William Hendriksen that in 1939 he titled his commentary on Revelation as *More than Conquerors*! At Rev 12:10ff we read that in Christ a great *victory* has been won and *"Now the salvation (sotēria, victory) and the power and the kingdom of our God and the authority of his Christ have come, for the accuser of our brethren has been thrown down...and they have conquered him by the blood of the Lamb and the word of their testimony..."*

In spite of the positive theme or theology of Revelation, it is in many ways a complicated book. There are several reasons for this:

*First*, it is an ancient book, written over 1900 years ago for people living in a foreign culture in what is today western Turkey.

*Second*, it comes to us in a strange language, style of writing using strange images, and a literary genre with which we are not very familiar. We will look into this in a later lesson.

*Third*, modern sensational millennial theories, for example, the *Left Behind* books of Tim LaHaye and Jerry B. Jenkins, have complicated the message and focused our attention in the wrong place or time. They push the message of Revelation in the wrong direction, toward the end of the world and away from the context of the Christians living in Asia at the close of the first century AD.

## So, what is Revelation All About?

As I mentioned above, for many today Revelation is a book about the end of the world, or the second coming of Jesus. Into this some have built the Rapture and Left Behind theories.

I would like to suggest to you that Revelation is *not* about the end of the world or about being left behind! This may come as a surprise to you since the fact that Revelation is not about the end of the world runs contrary to some popular theories of Revelation. Some speak about "the signs of the times," thinking that in Revelation we can find signs that predict the end of the world, but is this what Revelation is really all about?

Why not ask the person who wrote the book of Revelation, the Apostle John! *First*, some scholars have questioned the apostolic authorship of John. Nevertheless, it is the view of several fine, prominent and highly regarded scholars today that the book may well have been written by the Apostle John. If you need further information regarding this, refer to the commentaries listed above in the bibliography.

The best way to ask John what Revelation is all about is to refer to his opening comments in Revelation. It was a common literary feature of ancient writers like Paul and John to indicate in the opening verses of their writing what the central theme is which they will develop subsequently in their letter or book. So turn with me in your Bibles to Revelation 1:1-3. Notice how John begins this great book:

*"The revelation of Jesus Christ, which God gave him to show to his servants what must soon take place; and he made it known by sending his angel to his servant John ,$^2$who bore witness to the word of God and to the testimony of Jesus Christ, even to all that he saw. $^3$Blessed is he who reads aloud the words of the prophecy, and blessed are those who hear, and who keep what is written therein; for the time is near."*

We learn from this that Revelation is the revelation (the Greek word *apokalypsis* means *uncovering* or *revealing*) of a *message* from God through Jesus to God's servants. John is instructed to *bear witness* to the *message* of God, that is, the *word of God*, and the testimony concerning Jesus, indeed even to all that he has seen in the visions which he saw while on the Isle of Patmos (Rev 1:9) and write this message for the churches of Asia to read (Rev 1:4).

*First* I want to draw your attention to the clear statement in our text that this is a revelation of "what must **soon** take place"

(Rev 1:1). In your understanding of the English language, what does ***soon*** mean? Surely it means **soon**! However, let's see how your and other translations read this word. Most likely it is translated either *soon* or *shortly*! How does your translation read here? Cf. the KJV, ASV, NASV, NIV, RSV, NRSV, and the ESV. All of these translations read either ***soon*** or ***shortly***!

We should be able to understand from this that Revelation contains a message from God and Jesus about things that will (the Greek *dei* means *must* or *it is necessary to*) **soon** or **shortly** take place in the lives of the Christians in Asia! At least God and Jesus expected the things of Revelation to *soon* or *shortly* take place!

To this emphasis on an imminent expectation John adds a striking statement of urgency. The message is obviously urgent since it includes a message from the full godhead (Rev 1:3-6). Rev 1:3 adds to this sense of urgency the following point I wish to make.

*Second*, Rev 1:3 states that *the time is **near***. In your understanding of the English language, what does ***near*** normally mean? Surely it sounds something like ***soon*** or ***shortly***! However, the Greek expression for "the time is ***near***" is interesting in that technically it is a loaded term! We will learn in the next chapters that the literary context of Revelation is set in an apocalyptic eschatological context. We won't worry too much about the meaning of that expression at this point other than to emphasize that the word *time* in Greek is *kairos* which emphasizes *significant* time, *crisis* time, or *urgent* time. It does not simply mean the passing of time. In that case the Greek word for passing time is *chronos*, simply *time*! The sense of the Greek expression is that *a crisis time is imminent, soon, or about to break in on the churches*. One scholar in our bibliography has explained that the expression "the *time* is ***near***" includes an *exaggerated imminence*! This is a good explanation of the Greek expression. The message of Revelation is set in the context of event that will soon take place and John uses an expression of exaggerated imminence to draw attention to this.

Revelation is a book or letter written by John to the churches in Asia at God's instruction to warn the churches of an *impending crisis of persecution* that was *soon, near, shortly,* or *about to break in on them.*

Church history reinforces this by describing the extreme persecution experienced by the churches in Asia at the hands of the Roman Empire at the close of the 1st century and for the next 200 years. (Cf. Eusebius, *Ecclesiastical History*, vol. 1, and Frend, *Martyrdom and Persecution in the Early Church*. Both of these are referenced in our bibliography.)

## The Story of Revelation

We have learned from Rev 1:1-3 that certain things were ***soon*** to take place. They would create a ***crisis*** for the churches in Asia. We learn from our best church historians (e.g. Eusebius of Caesarea, ca. 330 AD, *Ecclesiastical History*, and W. H. C. Frend, *Martyrdom and Persecution in the Early Church*) that towards the close of the 1st century AD Christianity was seen by the Roman powers, and the pagan culture in which the churches lived, as a serious threat to Rome's stability and political domination.

Although at AD 96 we know of no Imperial Edict which instructed the Roman Provincial Governors to actively seek out Christians. However, the Christians' refusal to honor the Emperor or Caesar as a divine being, created problems for the saints. In Roman thinking this refusal was a treasonable threat to the Roman system and civil authority of Rome. Furthermore, the clashes between the Jews and the Christians over the divinity of Jesus became a major threat to Judaism. The break of Christians with the Temple, the Synagogue, and the Law reached a point of complete separation toward the close of the 1st century AD. By this time the Christians were perceived as a growing threat to both Judaism and Rome.

From several sectors, notably from the pagan world of Rome and from Synagogue Judaism, opposition began to escalate and plans to nullify or negate the Christian threat through persecution and social isolation broke out throughout the Roman Empire.

Because of these crises of faith, God in Revelation was warning the church that Satan would use the Imperial power of

Rome and the Roman religious Cult to demand obeisance or worship of the Roman Emperor as a sign of faithfulness to Rome.

Faithfulness to Jesus as the divine Son of God and ruler over His kingdom, and a denial of the divinity of the Roman Emperor brought Christians and the church into a direct clash with Rome, and continuing opposition from a Jewish Synagogue which was eager to grasp any means of destroying Christianity.

In view of this impending crisis and Imperial opposition God through the message of Revelation was calling the church and Christians to an uncompromising faith in Jesus. The message is "Jesus is Lord, not Caesar! Worship God, not Caesar!"

God knew that this uncompromising position would lead to persecution and in all possibility martyrdom, but as was the case with Jesus' death in faithfulness to God's will, God promised to transform the suffering and martyrdom of the saints into a magnificent victory. By dying for Christ, in one sense with Christ, the saints would reign completely with Christ in His kingdom. Although seemingly conquered by Satan and his powerful agent, Rome, the saints would become the conquerors through their faith in Jesus. The two texts that we have already referenced, Rev 12:10, 11 and Rom 8:37ff, are important to the message of revelation

In Revelation God wants the Christians to know that the real power behind Rome was Satan. It is clear throughout Revelation that the Emperor was nothing other than the agent of Satan. In Revelation Rome will be pictured in a variety of images including the Beast and the Harlot. The False Prophet in Revelation is representative of the Roman Imperial Cult that served the Imperial power of Rome through its religious Cult. The beast that comes up out of the sea (Rev 13) is identified as Leviathan, in this case symbolic of the Roman civil power, and the land beast that comes up out of the land is symbolic of Behemoth, the Imperial Religious Cult. We will learn at Rev 13 that these images of Leviathan and Behemoth are drawn from a rich Jewish tradition and heritage. Satan is pictured using these two symbolic beasts, especially the Imperial Cult as a direct challenge to the faith of the Christians.

The setting of Revelation is therefore the churches in Asia at the close of the 1$^{st}$ century AD facing the crisis of increasing

Roman, Jewish, and pagan opposition and oppression. The theology of message of Revelation is that of the immediate and ultimate *victory* of the church and Christians over Satan through their faith in Jesus and through Jesus' victory. The saints by dying for their faith in Jesus would be *more than conquerors in Christ* (Rom 8:37 ff; Rev 12:10-12.)

## What Can We Learn From This Chapter

- The book of Revelation is set in a first century AD historical context. Churches and Christians living in the Roman Province of Asia were faced with serious faith challenges. A series of crises involving oppression, persecution, and possibly martyrdom were already breaking into their daily lives. Although the theological principles involved in God's message to the seven churches are rooted in this first century context, the theological principles encountered are universal and applicable to all times and places. It is important, however, to first establish the original meaning of the message to those seven churches (seven being symbolic of all the churches in Asia), before translating them to contemporary contexts. Obviously great theological principles can be drawn from the message of Revelation that are applicable for Christians in all ages and all regions of the world.
- Satan has from the beginning of time been committed to destroying God's creation, especially mankind. He uses every possible vehicle in his seduction and temptation of men, tempting them to turn away from worshipping and honoring the one and only true God. In the case of the Christians in Asia Satan was using the awesome power of Rome, but Revelation explains that God will defeat Satan in this by removing Rome from the scene. Sometimes Satan uses people who should be God's people (in Revelation the Synagogue) as an agent of his seduction.
- The point of the message of Revelation is that Christians must constantly be alert to Satan's wiles. Satan tempts

people to prize life over faithfulness to God, hence the challenge of martyrdom for faith in Jesus. Those who succumb to the temptation to compromise do not realize that the life Satan offers is in reality ruin and destruction, whereas the death that Christians must choose (martyrdom) offers real life and victory in Christ. Through faithfulness to Christ Christians conquer Satan and reign with Jesus. Through dying for their faith Christians are more than conquerors.

## Our Next Chapter

In our next chapter we will briefly examine the Theology of Revelation and some practical lessons we can learn from Revelation for today!

## Homework

Read the following three texts; Dan 7; Psalm 2; Ezek 1:1-3:3.

# Chapter 2

# The Strange Language and Style of Revelation, and the Message of Revelation

## Introduction

In our first lesson we learned that Revelation is a message from God through Jesus to the churches in Asia about a crisis that was *soon* to break in on them. We learned that *soon* means *soon* and that *near* means *near*! We learned that the message or story of Revelation was about *victory in Christ* and being *more than conquerors in and through Christ.* As a reminder it would be good to reread Rom 8:35ff and Rev 12:10ff.

## Key Scriptures

**Rom 8:35ff.**

"Who shall separate us from the love of Christ? Shall tribulation, or distress, or persecution, or famine, or nakedness, or peril, or sword? $^{36}$ As it is written, "For thy sake we are being killed all the day long; we are regarded as sheep to be slaughtered." $^{37}$ No, in all these things we are more than conquerors through him who loved us. $^{38}$ For I am sure that neither death, nor life, nor angels, nor principalities, nor things present, nor things to come, nor powers, $^{39}$ nor height, nor depth, nor anything else in all creation, will be able to separate us from the love of God in Christ Jesus our Lord. "

**Rev 12:10ff.**

"And I heard a loud voice in heaven, saying, "Now the salvation and the power and the kingdom of our God and the authority of his Christ have come, for the accuser of our brethren has been thrown down, who accuses them day and night before our God. $^{11}$ And they have conquered him by the blood of the Lamb and by the word of their testimony, for they loved not their lives even unto death."

## The Importance of Three Major Texts to the Style and Theology of Revelation

Although the book of Revelation is found in the New Testament it is in many significant ways an Old Testament book! Scholars have estimated that John cites the Old Testament between 200 and 400 times in 22 chapters and approximately 404 verses! Without understanding the dynamic and symbolism of Old Testament Scriptures one will find it difficult to understand what John is doing in Revelation.

Three OT texts, however, will play a significant role in Revelation as John uses them to paint new visions and scenes.

*First*, Dan 7:1-28: We might call this the Son of Man text! The setting of this text in Daniel is of four beasts representing four kingdoms. We read also of the coming in clouds of one like *a Son of Man who will establish an everlasting kingdom.* The saints will receive the kingdom. The fourth beast with ten heads will produce a horn that will make war on the saints and speak against the Most High. *The horn will wear the saints out (persecute them) for 3 ½ years.* The horn will be judged and *the saints will reign in the everlasting kingdom.*

*Second*, Psalm 2: This is often identified as a Psalm of Kingly Ascent. Nations will conspire against God; Kingdoms will set themselves against the Lord and God's king. The Lord will hold them in derision and proclaim that he has set his king on Zion, the holy hill of Jerusalem. God will proclaim the King to be his son. *The king will be given a rod of iron with which to smash clay vessels.* The kings are warned to serve the Lord.

*Third*, Ezek 1:1-3:3: The Heavenly Scene and the Four Living Creatures conjure up heavenly scenes in Revelation. This text is set in Jewish *mystical (cosmic unearthly)* terms. Ezekiel is given a glimpse into heaven and sees *four living creatures who serve God.* He sees a strange chariot which goes in four different directions at the same time! This chariot with four strange wheels represents the mystery of the omnipresence and omniscience of God. *Ezekiel is commissioned to go and preach. He is given a scroll to eat that is sweet in his mouth implying that the message of the scroll is sweet and good.*

Several of the expressions italicized in the above three texts resonate throughout Revelation.

## The Mysterious Style of Revelation

It does not take long when reading Revelation before we realize that its language and symbolism are strange, at least to our modern western manner of thinking!

*First of all*, as noted in the previous chapter this is a different kind of New Testament book. In many ways it sounds like and OT book! John incorporates a brilliant collage of OT Scriptures to tell his story. While the OT texts or references may not be that meaningful to us they certainly would have been to John's readers whose Bible was most likely the Septuagint or Greek version of the OT since most of the NT books had not yet been widely circulated or collected into the codex or book which we call the New Testament. John uses the OT references as symbols to paint the scenes described in Revelation. In addition to the OT John incorporates references to the large Jewish corpus of apocalyptic, apocryphal, and pseudepigraphical library with which the Christians would surely have been familiar. I will say more about this genre of literature below.

My point here is that unless we know the stories of the OT well and how the OT symbols John uses call to memory divine principles we will have difficulty understanding Revelation. Indicating an excellent knowledge of the OT stories and symbols and in a brilliant demonstration of literary skill John uses these OT "colors" to paint his brilliant scenes revealed to him by God through the Holy Spirit.

Old Testament books that are particularly important to Revelation are Daniel, Ezekiel, Zechariah, Psalms, Isaiah, and Jeremiah. The plagues on Egypt in Exodus also play an important role in the latter portion of Revelation.

*Second*, Revelation is a *highly figurative and symbolic* book using Jewish idiom and images that we do not always understand very well. The numbers John uses draw on a rich Jewish symbolic system. In keeping with the style of Revelation the numbers, images, and literary genre are highly symbolic, and without a keen sensitivity to this symbolism interpreters tend to be overly literal and interpret the message of Revelation beyond its real style and message.

*Third*, John draws heavily on what we call an *apocalyptic* style with which today are we are most unfamiliar. Apocalyptic literature and the apocalyptic genre are intentionally highly symbolic, intending to draw the reader's eye and mind beyond the physical into the spiritual. Apocalyptic literature was the literature of Jews and Christians living under severe persecution and oppression. This kind of literature is found in what we call the Apocryphal and Pseudepigraphal literature of Judaism and Christianity. With their roots in the political and religious upheavals of Israel ca. 200 B.C. and continuing into the Judeo/Christian era until ca. 200 A.D, this literature focused hope not on political power but on Divine intervention into human affairs. John draws heavily on the images and figures in this literature since they were familiar to his readers. Typical of this genre (kind) of literature are: *Tobit, Baruch,* 1, 2 *Enoch, Sibylline Oracles, Testament of Levi, Wisdom of Solomon,* 1, 2, 3 *Maccabees*, and many others.

The apocalyptic mindset is extremely pessimistic about human potential and ability to solve the issues of oppression, persecution, and suffering, so it resorts to looking to God's divine intervention to resolve its concerns. Apocalyptic literature presents its story in cosmic visions with many angels and demonic beings that are at war with the saints. The vast library of apocalyptic texts ranged over a period beginning ca. 200 B.C. and lasting until ca. 200 A.D. This covered the establishment and spread of the church in a hostile Jewish and Roman environment. John resorts to this highly symbolic library of thought and to the dramatic symbols of the OT as he builds his story of oppression, persecution, faith, and victory.

# John's Use of the Eschatological Genre in Revelation

We noticed in the first chapter of this commentary that Revelation is not about the end of the world but is all about a series of crises and challenges to faith that the churches in Asia were about to face. In fact the clash with the Synagogue and Rome had already begun and John tells us that a Christian, Antipas, in Pergamum had already died as a martyr. We will say more about this in a later chapter on the seven churches in Asia, Rev 2 and 3. The point is that although Revelation is not about the end of the world John repeatedly resorts to end of the world language to tell his story! We call this end of the world terminology eschatological language.

Eschatology is a unique way of looking at time and the world. It was not strange to Christians and Jews but Gentiles would not normally have thought of time and the world in this manner. Typically, many Gentiles saw time as cyclical without beginning and end. However the Judeo/Christian world view was that the world and time had a beginning and would also have an end. They believed that God created everything in the beginning and would bring it all to a close sometime in the future. The decision as to when the end would come was God's, for God was working his plan of redemption for his creation in time and history. The technical term for this plan of salvation or redemption in which God is redeeming his creation from sin is *Heilsgeschichte.* This is a German term that literally means salvation history. In theological terms it means that God is working his plan of salvation in history.

The term eschatology is derived from two Greek words, *eschatos* and *logos*. *Eschatos* means final, end, or last. Logos has a wide variety of meanings including word, discussion, message, and proclamation. Eschatology is understood to reference discussion, dialogue, or message about final things. This can mean either *temporal final things* or *significant things*. The Jews looked for a final event, the coming of a messiah figure who would restore God's reign to Israel and the world. We might call this an *eschatological hope*.

Christians understood the end to have begun when Jesus came into the world and began his messianic ministry. Note the following texts:

**Matt 12:28.** When Jesus was accused of casting out demons by the power of Be-elzebul, the prince of demons, he responded "But if it is by the Spirit of God that I cast out demons, *then the kingdom of God has come upon you.*"

**Acts 2:17.** On the day of Pentecost when the Holy Spirit fell on the apostles resulting in their speaking in tongues the crowd accused them of being drunk. Peter responded that they were not drunk, "but this is what was spoken by the prophet Joel: [17] '*And in the last days it shall be, God declares, that I will pour out my Spirit upon all flesh...*"

**Heb 1:1, 2.** The writer of the Letter to the Hebrews opens his "sermon" regarding the supremacy of Jesus with this remark, "In many and various ways God spoke of old to our fathers by the prophets; [2] but *in these last days he has spoken to us by a Son*, whom he appointed the heir of all things, through whom also he created the world."

It is apparent that Jesus, Luke, and the author of the Hebrew Epistle understood that the last days had begun in the ministry of Jesus, and in fact had therefore been inaugurated. (Inaugurated Eschatology is a technical term indicating that the end has begun in Jesus. In fact, one prominent New Testament theologian observed that Jesus is the crucial turning point in time, having inaugurated the end or last days.)

Inaugurated eschatology, which John obviously adopts in his fascinating style of writing Revelation, understands that any event in the last days, the days between the ministry of Jesus and his return (second coming) can be and should be described in end of the world language since the end of the world, the last days, has already begun. Every decision Christians make in the last days has end of the world significance and consequences!

John adapts this inaugurated eschatological style to explain that the challenges to Christian faith, breaking in on the churches in Asia, has end-of-the world significance, as do their response to those challenges. Those whose faith is compromised by worship of the Emperor need to know that their loss of faith has end of the world consequences. They also need to know that their enemies have already been judged by God with end of the world finality and consequences.

Thus when it seems like John is speaking of the end of the world he is doing so dramatically and symbolically, demonstrating the seriousness of the event he is describing. Those who understood the apocalyptic genre would also understand this inaugurated eschatological genre. The combination of these apocalyptic and eschatological genres we call apocalyptic eschatology.

Because the apocalyptic/eschatological genre is so highly symbolic and therefore projects its message onto a cosmic scene, and because it is pessimistic about human endeavor such as political intervention to solve the believer's problems and looks for God's divine intervention into human affairs, it is important to remember to interpret such language in Revelation in the context of the oppression and suffering of the Christians in the first century A.D. The interpreter must look back into the history of the Old Testament Scriptures and the apocalyptic literature in order to understand the symbolism adopted by John in Revelation. The relationship between Old Testament and apocalyptic texts is not one of an historical temporal fulfillment but one of an analogous or typological fulfillment. We look for what the Old Testament or apocalyptic message was and find an analogous application of this to John's historical context. Once we have done that we follow the same principle of determining the theological principle John is communicating to his audience and explore ways in which we can apply that theological principle to our context in an analogous manner.

Those of us in our modern western culture who are not familiar with either apocalyptic or eschatology have difficulty understanding John's use of end of the world language and tend to literalize this. We must keep in mind John's unique and stylish use of this familiar Judeo/Christian genre as he tells his story to the first century Christians in Asia.

## John's Literary Genius

We have already noticed that Revelation is significantly influenced by both the Old Testament and Jewish literature such as the Apocrypha, Pseudepigrapha, and Apocalyptic tradition. Skillfully John blends these traditions into a powerful message of struggle, hope, and victory. His cosmic images are enriched by his literary and theological genius. Demonstrating a remarkable literary acumen John links his visions and scenes together with link words that tie the message together as John moves from seven seals revealed from a great scroll which represents God's plan for dealing with the problem of evil. He adroitly moves from the message to the seven churches in Asia, connecting to seven seals through seven trumpets, seven angelic messages, seven bowls of wrath, to God's judgment on Rome and finally His judgment of the beast, false prophet, and then Satan himself.

Attempting to discern some form of structure has challenged scholars since the third century of the Christian era when Victorinus of Pettau wrote what to our knowledge was the first commentary written on Revelation. Victorinus made a significant observation that themes in Revelation were repeated throughout the book. His concept was identified as *recapitulatio* a Latin term meaning recapitulation or repeating. Explaining the relationship of these recapitulated themes has resulted in the modern era in what we call *chiasm* or a *chiastic* structure. William Hendriksen in his important commentary, *More Than Conquerors*, described this recapitulation as a *progressive parallelism* in which themes are repeated in a progressive style in parallel form. Today several scholars have identified a chiastic structure in this literary form. Chiasm is the first or left hand side of the letter chi, best illustrated in our letter X. The diagram below and the model of chiasm we will follow in Revelation will illustrate this chiastic style.

In this literary structure, point **A** of the structure leads to point **B**, to **C**, and then to the climax or final point **D**. The movement then goes back to **C1**, to **B1**, to **A1**. **A** and **A1** are parallel, **B** and **B1** are parallel, and so forth.

The intention of a chiastic structure is to lead the reader through progressive steps to a climax or main point of the discussion. The diagrams below will illustrate a chiastic structure and demonstrate the parallelism of the structure.

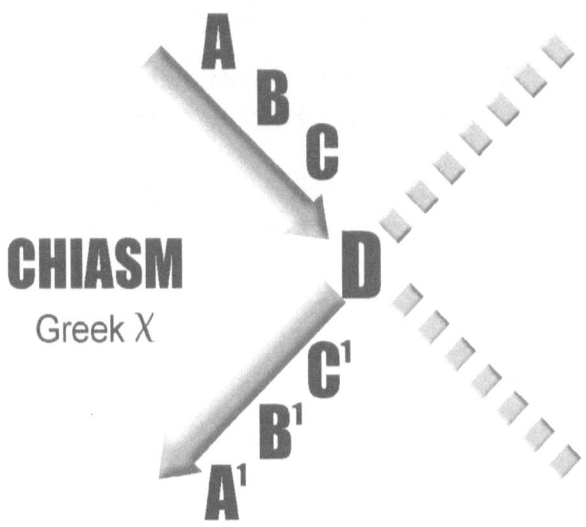

Prologue 1:1-20
I. The Church in Imperfection. 2:1-3:22
   Seven Letters to the Seven Churches
    II. The Authority of God over Evil Explained. 4:1-8:6
      Seven Seals on the Scroll
       III. The Warning Judgments. 8:1-11:19
         Seven Trumpets
          IV. The Lamb - God's Answer to Evil. 12:1-14:20
           Seven Unnumbered Figures
        V. The Consummated Judgments. 15:1-16:21
         Seven Bowls of Wrath
    VI. The Authority of God over Evil Exercised. 17:1-20:15
      Seven Unnumbered Descriptions of God's Judgments
VII. The Church in Perfection. 21:1-22:5
   Seven Unnumbered Descriptions of the Church in Perfection
Epilogue 22:6-21

In this study we will draw on the terminology of a scholar in the field of revelation, Austin Farrer, and refer to the *recapitulatio* style of John as a *rebirth of images* in which an image is presented and then successively repeated and developed (reborn) each time adding to the meaning of the term.

## What We Learn from this and the Previous Chapter

- We learn first of all that God knows about and cares for his churches. He understands their crises, strengths, and weaknesses.
- He therefore warns his church that because of Jesus they will face a challenge to their faith.
- He encourages them to get their faith sorted out before crises strike them.
- Rom 8:37ff and Rev 12:10, 11 stress the fact that in Christ we are more than conquerors and that we have already defeated Satan through our resolute faith in Jesus.
- We have noticed that Revelation is a mysterious book to us because of its age, historical and literary contexts, and adoption of an apocalyptic/eschatological genre to convey its message of hope to those who keep faith in God's plan of redemption which is focused in Jesus.
- Because the apocalyptic genre is so symbolic we should be careful not to interpret apocalyptic concepts in Revelation literally but should seek to understand the theology of the message.
- Jesus stressed that the kingdom had already begun in his ministry, and both Luke and the writer of the Hebrew Epistle stated clearly that the last days had already begun.
- John adopts such an inaugurated eschatological genre and use of end of the world terminology to explain that present issues such as an uncompromising or compromised faith both have end of the world significance.
- It is important when working with highly symbolic literature such as Old Testament prophecy, the apocalyptic genre, and inaugurated eschatology to look for theological principles that can be carried forward form one historical context to another.

## Our Next Chapter

In our next chapter we will explore the theology of Revelation. We will again stress the importance of identifying theological principles which can apply to our contemporary context.

Knowing the story of Revelation is important as it is set in the $1^{st}$ century of the churches in Asia, but knowing the theological message and principles of this great book are equally important for understanding how relevant this book is for today.

# Chapter 3

# Introduction to the Theology and Relevant Lessons of Revelation

## Revelation is a Narrative Set in the Context of a Clash of Wills between Satan and his Agent, Rome and the Churches in Asia

We noticed in Chapter 1 of this commentary, when observing the importance of Rev 1:1-3 for setting the scene of Revelation, that God through Jesus was revealing to John and the churches in Asia *things that must soon take place,* for a *crisis time was about to break in on the church.* John used the loaded eschatological expression of *the time is near* to stress in *exaggerated imminence* the *urgency* of the situation facing the churches in Asia and the message of Revelation. As Revelation unfolds John will draw on several images, some significantly apocalyptic, to dramatize this clash which in true apocalyptic form he describes as a war with Satan and the forces of evil. One that stands out is his description of a war that broke out in heaven between the archangel Michael and his angelic force and the dragon, Satan, and his demonic force. Satan is defeated and forced out of heaven and thrown down to earth to carry out his battle against God's creation (Rev 12:7ff). Another dramatic figure is of Satan calling an evil beast out of the sea (the sea is a sources of evil in Hebrew mythology). This beast a symbol of Rome makes war on the saints and conquers them (Rev 13:1ff). We will learn later that by conquering, that is killing the saints; Satan is himself defeated and conquered by their faith, the essence of Christian martyrdom. Rev 11:7ff tells of the beast making war on the saints and killing them. Those who worship the beast rejoice in this and refuse to let the slain saints be buried. However, a breath of God enters the slain saints and they are raised into heaven to celebrate their victory with God. Adela Yarbro Collins in an excellent study, *Combat Mythology in the Book of Revelation*, observes that the primary context in which we should view Revelation, and interpret it, is of a war between Satan and God's Church. Revelation is replete with this same theme of a war fought by Satan against the church.

The message of Revelation is one of resolute faith in Jesus and victory over Satan through an uncompromising faith which in many cases would result inevitably in martyrdom. This theme resonates throughout Revelation in a number of different visions and themes. The message is one of *tribulation, faithfulness* and *reigning with Christ*.

As he begins to build his theme at Rev 1:9 John informed the Christians in Asia that he shared with them in *tribulation*, the *kingdom*, and *patient endurance*. He was on the island of Patmos, a penal colony, a prisoner of Rome on account of the word (message) of God and his testimony concerning Jesus. Understanding the symbiotic relationship between these three concepts, *tribulation, patient endurance,* and *kingdom* is vital to understanding the message and theology of Revelation. The point of the message is that by *faithfully enduring tribulation* (persecution) the saints would *conquer* Satan and *reign* with Jesus in his eternal *kingdom*. A major thrust of Revelation is that the combination of two major themes, the death of Jesus and his victory over Satan in his resurrection, combined with the faithful martyrdom of the saints, secures victory for the saints over Satan. One is reminded that Paul in Rom 8:1-6 had assured the Roman Christians that by being baptized into Christ they were united with him in both his death and resurrection. In one sense they had already died to this life and risen to a new life. Martyrdom is an analogy to this death and resurrection through being united with Christ in his victory over Satan. In one sense baptism is a proleptic experience of the final death and resurrection of every Christian. In the same manner martyrdom is *a proleptic experience* of the final death and resurrection.

I have introduced you to a new expression that is important to understanding Revelation! A *proleptic experience*! *Proleptic* derives from two Greek words, *pro* which means before or in advance, *leptic* derives from *lēmpsomai* meaning to receive. A proleptic experience is to experience something before the final experience! For instance baptism is a proleptic experience of the resurrection to life at the end of the age. The Lord's Supper is a proleptic experience of the final heavenly banquet when all of God's people will sit with him at his heavenly table and be sustained by God and his presence. Martyrdom and the resurrection of the martyrs to be with Jesus and sit on his throne (a theme that we will develop at Rev 2, 3) is a *proleptic experience* of the final judgment and resurrection to be with God and Jesus in heaven. Remember, Revelation is full of symbolism!

## Revelation is a Narrative of Victory and Conquering

William Hendriksen in the 1950s accurately titled his commentary on Revelation *More Than Conquerors*. He adapted the title from Romans 8: 37-39 with an emphasis on vs. 37. To be reminded again of the importance of this text and Rev 12:10ff we need to read them again carefully.

"What then shall we say to this? If God is for us, who is against us? [32] He who did not spare his own Son but gave him up for us all, will he not also give us all things with him? [33] Who shall bring any charge against God's elect? It is God who justifies; [34] who is to condemn? Is it Christ Jesus, who died, yes, who was raised from the dead, who is at the right hand of God, who indeed intercedes for us? [35] Who shall separate us from the love of Christ? Shall tribulation, or distress, or persecution, or famine, or nakedness, or peril, or sword? [36] As it is written, "For thy sake we are being killed all the daylong; we are regarded as sheep to be slaughtered." [37] No, *in all these things we are more than conquerors through him who loved us.* [38] For I am sure that neither death, nor life, nor angels, nor principalities, nor things present, nor things to come, nor powers, [39] nor height, nor depth, nor anything else in all creation, will be able to separate us from the love of God in Christ Jesus our Lord."

Turn to Rev 12:10, 11 and read these magnificent verses with me. They form the climax of the theology of Revelation:

> "Now war arose in heaven, Michael and his angels fighting against the dragon; and the dragon and his angels fought, [8] but they were defeated and there was no longer any place for them in heaven. [9] And the great dragon was thrown down, that ancient serpent, who is called the Devil and Satan, the deceiver of the whole world—he was thrown down to the earth, and his angels were thrown down with him. [10] And I heard a loud voice in heaven, saying, *"Now the salvation and the power and the kingdom of our God and the authority of his Christ have come, for the accuser of our brethren has been thrown down, who accuses them day and night before our God. [11] And they have conquered him by the blood of the Lamb and by the word of their testimony, for they loved not their lives even unto death.* [12] Rejoice then, O heaven and you that dwell therein! But woe to you, O earth and sea, for the devil has come down to you in great wrath, because he knows that his time is short!"

Although the message of Revelation resonates with images that stress that Satan is at war with the church, the message also resonates with the theme that Christians can *conquer* (*overcome*, NIV) Satan through their resolute faithfulness to Jesus. The Christians faith works in conjunction with Jesus' death and resurrection providing them with a triumphant victory over Satan. *As Paul wrote in encouragement of Christians in Rome, we are more than conquerors through him who loved us!*

A surprising shift in emphasis is found at Rev 11:15ff. This scene is of the sounding of the seventh and last trumpet of judgment on Rome. One expects a scene stressing the details of God's judgment on Rome, but in a striking twist of John's kaleidoscope of visions we see the twenty four elders who sit on thrones in God's throne room praising God for exercising his kingdom reign through Christ. God is praised for taking his great power, rewarding the saints for their faithfulness, and destroying the destroyers!

The message and theology of Revelation is clearly one of *Victory* and *Conquering in Christ*. It is also a message calling on Christians to remain true to Christ, maintaining faith in Christ, keeping Christ at the center of faith, and not compromising faith with a pagan world.

## Revelation Calls on Christians to Focus Their Faith on God and His Holiness, Righteousness, and Sovereignty

Almost from the beginning of his message John reminds the saints to see God in all of His sovereign power.

At Rev 1:4 John draws attention to the eternal God who is creator of everything. In his own stylistic manner he cites Ex 3:14 where God tells Moses that He is the I AM who, that is the eternal God. John's words in revelation are that God is the one "*who is and who was and who is to come*"! In Rev 4 John, in like manner to Isaiah (Isa 6) and Ezekiel (Ezek 1), is transported in a vision into the Heavenly Throne Room, right into the presence of the Almighty, Holy God. Four living creatures and twenty four elders sing the praises of God, Holy, Holy, Holy, is the Lord God Almighty, who was and is and is to come…worthy art thou, our Lord and God, to receive glory and honor, and power, for thou didst create all things, and by thy will they existed and were created."

Such themes are repeated throughout Revelation as the saints are encouraged to focus their faith on the Holiness, Sovereignty, and Righteousness of God. This message is important to the *theodicy* of Revelation (a defense of the righteousness of God in the presence of evil).

In a fascinating scene in Rev 4, in the Heavenly Throne Room of God, we see a sea, glasslike like crystal! In Hebrew and Near Eastern mythology the sea was understood to be one of the origins of evil. The bottomless pit was another. However in the Throne Room in the presence of the Almighty God, the sea is calm and plays no role at all. John wants Christians to understand that evil in the presence of God is harmless. As John concludes his triumphant message at Rev21:1, after Satan and his henchmen have been judged and cast into the lake of fire, evil is no more! The Sovereign Ruler of the world has exercised his great power and in righteousness has vindicated and rewarded his faithful saints.

Throughout Revelation John wants the saints never to lose sight of the Holiness, Sovereignty, and Righteousness of God.

## What We Can Learn for Today from Revelation

- We have learned previously that Revelation is not about the end of the world.
- It is about a war set in the context of the churches in Asia in the first century AD.
- However the theological principles seen in this message are ageless and apply to our contemporary contexts as deeply as it applied to the first century churches.
- It speaks of an ageless war between Satan and God's purpose that takes place in first century AD Asia.
- The story is one of suffering for one's faith in Jesus and consequently conquering through that resolute faith.
- Revelation speaks in end of the world eschatological language because the last days have already begun.
- Revelation has end of the world implications in that our present decisions are judged by God with the end of the world significance.
- God warns Christians in advance that life will be filled with difficulties and suffering.
- Satan will do everything in his power to get Christians to compromise their faith in Jesus with the world.
- We are reminded in Revelation that God is in control of his creation and world and will provide an escape from Satan and his power through Jesus' victory over Satan in his death, burial, and resurrection.
- Christians are called to an uncompromising faith in Jesus.

- It is always Jesus who must be the center of Christian faith, not the church, not Scripture, not doctrine, not good works.
- Christians must work through understanding God's *Holiness*, *Sovereignty*, and *Righteousness*.
- Christians may be called to die for their faith in Jesus, but the reward for faithfulness far outweighs the cost.
- Satan and those who choose to take his side will be held accountable by God and judged by God in God's time according to his plan.
- God has an eternal plan (*Heilsgeschichte*) and is working that plan. We must be faithful and patient and trust in God as He works his plan.

## Our Next Chapter

In chapter 4 we will enter the textual study of Revelation by examining the Prologue to the book. In typical "Johannine" style John includes a Prologue and Epilogue which serve as "bookends" to the story. Messages and thoughts, even some precise words in the Prologue, are repeated in the Epilogue which technically explains that the message and theological themes of Revelation are revealed in the Prologue and concluded in the Epilogue.

# Chapter 4

# The Prologue of Revelation:

# Revelation 1

## Introduction

As we observed in the previous chapter Revelation has a Prologue (Rev 1:1-20) and Epilogue (Rev 22:6-21) in which John repeats the major emphases and theological concerns of Revelation. Two key texts of the Prologue and Epilogue highlight the context and theology of Revelation, Rev 1:1-3 *"What must soon take place...for the time is near"* and Rev 22:6, 10 *"What must soon take place...for the time is near."* Notice how these two themes are repeated illustrating that these two themes form the context in which Revelation should be interpreted.

This type of literary construction in which words or themes are repeated at the beginning of a sentence, paragraph, chapter, or book we call an *inclusio* which sets boundaries to the discussion and defines what the message is. An *inclusio* serves as gates to a discussion that closes the meaning of the discussion between the two gates. We should conclude from this that Revelation is about a *crisis* which is *about to break in on the churches in Asia.* In this context God through Jesus and John warned the church of the impending crisis about to break in on them and encouraged the saints to endure faithfully, even unto death

Rev 1 as the prologue to the book sets the scene for, and defines the message of Revelation. Understanding the Prologue is vitally important to interpreting Revelation for in it John will explain what Revelation is all about. We noticed in the first chapter of this commentary that Revelation is not about the end of the world but speaks of crises that are about to (an exaggerated imminence) break into the lives of the churches in Asia. Paying careful attention to Rev 1:1-3 is vital to the interpretation of Revelation. We will have another detailed look at this text below.

## The Contents of the Prologue

We will note that the prologue is divided into three sections:
1. The Source of the Revelation (Rev 1:1-3) which explains that the message comes directly from God through Jesus and John.
2. The Salutation to the churches (Rev 1:4-8) in which John draws attention to the involvement of the full godhead or trinity in this message.
3. The Voice and The Vision of Jesus (Rev 1:9-20) in which John gives the readers a magnificent vision or description of the triumphant Jesus.

## The Source of the Revelation (Rev 1:1-3)

This brief text sets the scene for the story of Revelation! Revelation is a message of the *revelation* of a crisis that comes from God through Jesus and angels to God's servant John (Rev 1:1, 2). John Uses the Greek word *apokalypsis* to describe the book as a revelation. *Apokalypsis* simply means an *uncovering* or *revealing* of a message. This message is important since it comes directly from God through Jesus and angels to John. Angels are involved in important messages from God, as in the case of the Law of Moses (cf. Gal 3:19). We will comment on John below but he must have been an important and well respected person in the life of the Churches in Asia for God to choose him as the vehicle of this message.

Rev 1:1. God stresses that this message involves "*what must soon take place*". The Greek word translated *must* is a strong word, *dei*, which stresses *compulsion, necessity,* or *inevitability*. The Greek adverbial expression translated *soon* is *en tachei* which means *without delay, at once, soon, speedily*. All major translations of the English Bible translate this as either *soon* (RSV, NIV, NAS, or *shortly* (KJV, NKJV, NAS). This is not a message about the end of the world but one about things that are *inevitable*, that will *soon take place* in the lives of the churches in Asia.

Rev 1:3 emphasizes the *urgency* of the message. Each of the verbal forms in this verse is in the presence tense implying *repeated action*. God pronounces a blessing on those who *constantly read* the message of Revelation *aloud* (the Greek word *anaginōskō* means *public reading* in the congregation) and those who *constantly hear* and *constantly keep* the message. These present tenses add to the urgency and *importance* of the message. You get the idea that God wants the Christians to hear this message, and pay attention to it! The expression *for the time is near* is loaded with meaning! The words John uses are words found commonly in eschatological contexts that stress the significance of the time involved. First, he uses the word *kairos* for time. The normal word for time is *chronos* which signifies *mere time as it passes*. *Kairos* carries the sense of *significant time or crisis time*. John is drawing attention to *a crisis that is imminent*. This ties in well to the expression *soon* in Rev 1:1. The word translated near is from *eggus* means *close by* or *imminent*. When set in an *eschatological* context (remember John uses an *inaugurated eschatological* genre to tell his story in Revelation) *kairos* and *eggus* carry the sense of *imminent certainty*. As mentioned in the introductory chapter 2 one prominent scholar speaks here of an *exaggerated or heightened imminence*. The *crisis time* is so *near it is about to break in on them*.

Revelation is a message about a crisis that is both *inevitable* because of the faith of the Christians and *imminent* because of religio-political issues developing in Asia between Rome, the Synagogue, and the Church.

## The Salutation (Rev 1:4-8)

Rev 1:4. Revelation is a message from God and Jesus through John to the *seven* churches of Asia. Like all the books of the New Testament Revelation was written to a specific context and situation. Significant theological principles are developed which although originally addressed to the churches of the first century AD in Asia have universal and timeless implications. It is our task to determine what these theological principles are and how to translate them to our context.

We know that there were more than seven churches in Asia at the time of writing (we know of at least 16 churches in the Roman province of Asia at the close of the first century AD), so why *seven churches*? Simply because this is Revelation and things get done in sevens in Revelation! *Seven* was a special number in Judaism that symbolized both *holiness* and *completeness*. This is a message for *all the churches in Asia that belong to God.*

The salutation contains a prayer greeting, *Grace* and *peace* from the eternal God – *He who is, was, and is to come, from* the Holy Spirit – *the seven spirits before the throne*, and from Jesus Christ – *the faithful witness, the first born of the dead, and the ruler of kings* (Rev 1:5). *Grace* is a prayer for God's *favor*, and *peace* relates to a spirit of *inner tranquility and strength*.

Rev 1:6. John introduces a concept or theme that is of significance to the theology of Revelation. Jesus has made us a kingdom and priests to his God and Father. Being a kingdom and being priests will resonate throughout Revelation. Through faith in Jesus that inevitably leads to martyrdom the saints are promised by Jesus that they will sit on thrones with him. Thrones imply reigning and a kingdom! The martyrs will reign with Jesus in his kingdom (a message that reaches its climax at Rev 20:4)! John will explain that dying as a martyr is to be seen as offering one's life as a sacrifice in honor of God. Christians are thus a kingdom and priests. This is not a new concept as Peter also draws on this imagery at 1 Pet 2:9, "But you are a chosen race, *a royal priesthood*, a holy nation, God's own people, that you may declare the wonderful deeds..." In another context (Ex 19:6) God through Moses had promised to Israel "*you shall be to me a kingdom of priests and a holy nation.*" John closes this verse with a doxological like statement, "*to him be glory and dominion for ever and ever.*" A point John will make throughout Revelation is that dominion and power belong to Jesus.

Rev 1:7. In his typical use of the Old Testament John draws on Zech 12:10 where Zechariah predicts great mourning in Jerusalem over God's judgment of the city. Here John refers to Jesus who will come in the clouds to both save and judge. The message of Revelation includes both concepts; salvation or victory and judgment on those who compromise their faith in Jesus and those who persecute God's people. The vindication of the saints for their faithful suffering and martyrdom, and God's judgment on those who oppose His purpose and persecute His people are prominent themes throughout Revelation.

Rev 1:8. John closes the salutation by returning to his emphasis in Rev 1:1 on God, the Almighty, the beginning and the end, the eternal one. This little doxology emphasizes the importance and authority of the message.

## The Voice and the Vision (Rev 1:9-20)

In this section we highlight two important aspects of the message of Revelation. The message is without question important since it comes directly from Jesus! John will first hear a loud voice like a trumpet. Loud messages and mighty angels imply an important and urgent message. This is followed by a striking image of Jesus, not of an emaciated body hanging on a cross or a baby in his mother's arms (both important messianic images in other contexts), but of a triumphant warrior. We are reminded that Revelation is set in Combat Mythology (cf. Adela Yarbro Collins).

## The Voice (Rev 1:9-11)

Rev 1:9. John is on the island of Patmos, which was a prison for political prisoners, on account of the word of God, most likely to be interpreted as his message concerning Jesus. Obviously he has taught that Jesus is the only divine Lord, not Caesar, and this has been interpreted as treasonable. John introduces the theme of *suffering tribulation* (persecution), *patient endurance* (resolute faith) and *the kingdom* (reign of Jesus). These three are a trilogy of concepts that are vital to understanding the message of Revelation. Through suffering faithfully through oppression and persecution, even dying for that faith, the saints will reign with Jesus in his kingdom. This little trilogy is an example of John's rebirth of images concept as he introduces a concept and develops it incrementally as he works though Revelation.

Rev 1:10. John was on the Island of Patmos on the Lord's Day in a spiritual condition when Jesus spoke to him in a commanding voice like a trumpet, obviously intended to imply an important message. Jesus tells John to write to the seven churches of Asia: Ephesus, Smyrna, Pergamum, Thyatira, Sardis, Philadelphia, and Laodicea (Rev 1:11). These churches are representative of all churches, not only in Asia, but throughout the world even today!

## The Vision (Rev 1:12-20)

This vision is vital to the message of Revelation and John will repeatedly come back to the images of the vision as he writes to the seven churches and introduces Jesus to them. The vision was obviously one of a triumphant and victorious reigning Jesus, not a dead Jesus, but a conquering Lord.

Rev 1:13. Jesus is described as one like the son of man, drawing thoughts from Dan 7:13 where one like a son of man conquers the beast and receives an eternal kingdom.

Rev 1:13-16. Jesus is robed in divine regalia drawn from the OT. In his right hand he holds seven stars which seemingly represent the eternal destiny of the churches (Rev 1:16). Jesus, not Caesar, holds the eternal destiny of the churches!

Rev 1:17-20. Like Isaiah (Isa 6:4, 5) John falls down in reverence and awe at Jesus' feet as though he were dead.

Jesus tells John not to fear and then describes himself in divine terms as the first and the last. Jesus explains that he is the living one *who died and came to life for evermore* (Rev 1:18), a theme that is vital to those who are being called on to die as martyrs for their faith. The God who raised Jesus from the dead will also raise the martyrs from the dead to reign with Jesus. Jesus, not Caesar, holds the keys (authority) over Death and Hades (Hades from the Greek *hadēs* is a symbol of the place of the dead. It does not mean hell).

Jesus instructs John to write what he sees, that is, what is now taking place and what will soon take place (Rev 1:19).

Technically this should be translated as *"write what you see, that is, what is now happening and what is about to take place."*

The seven golden lampstands represent the seven churches (Rev 1:12, 20). Jesus explains that the stars in his hand are angels (who represent the seven churches) and the lampstands are churches (Rev 1:20).

## What We Learn From This Chapter and the Prologue

- God was concerned for his people and was warning them, in advance, that life will not be without serious problems.
- Several crises would soon break in on the churches in Asia. This principle of life being challenged by crises is true to all history. He calls us to constantly read, here, and keep his word (message).
- God through Jesus was setting the scene for the crises to be faced by the churches in Asia.
- There is a sense of urgency in the message of Revelation.
- The message comes from the full godhead; the Eternal God, the Holy Spirit, and Jesus Christ the King of kings.
- John informs us that Jesus and our faithful relationship with him has made us into a kingdom of priests who offer sacrifices to God. In the context of Revelation, our sacrifices are our own lives.
- In order to understand the significance of the message one must see Jesus described in all his full divine glory and authority. In his magnificent vision of Jesus John does this very thing! We see Jesus regnant and triumphant.
- Jesus is the one who died and is risen and who lives forever. He has secured our resurrection and eternal life with God.
- Because of his resurrection and reigning as king over God's kingdom Jesus has the keys or power over death and the realm of the dead. This power does not reside in Caesar or any other human power.

- Jesus calls on Christians to die faithfully to him with the promise that he will raise them up and they will live and reign forever with him in his eternal kingdom.
- We are reminded that in order to understand Revelation we must know the Old Testament and its images.
- We are again called on to think seriously about the Holiness, Sovereignty, and Righteousness of God, especially as we see Jesus in his sovereign and divine power.

## Our Next Chapter

This next chapter will be a study of the seven churches, their strengths and weaknesses, and Jesus' message to them. The seven churches are representative of all the churches in Asia, and but they are representative of churches throughout the ages, even today!

# Chapter 5

# The Seven Letters to the Seven Churches: Revelation 2 & 3

## Introduction

We have noted at Rev 1:4 that Revelation was addressed to "the seven churches that are in Asia". Seven was one of the many numbers John adopted from the rich symbolic Jewish tradition. Seven is a holy number that among other things represents completeness. We know that when John wrote Revelation there were already possibly 16 churches in the Roman Province of Asia. The message of Revelation was intended for all the churches in Asia. We will note, however, that the seven messages of Rev 2 and 3 speak to all churches in all ages.

The seven churches addressed are Ephesus, Smyrna, Pergamum, Thyatira, Sardis, Philadelphia, and Laodicea (Rev 1:11). Identifying the message of Revelation with real churches adds a sense of reality and historicity to the problem being addressed by God in Revelation. Ephesus was the cultural center of Asia, and Pergamum the Roman capital of the province of Asia. The other churches one might see as typical of the broad church scene in Asia

Of the seven churches *five were rebuked* for improper faith, and called on by Jesus to repent. Should they not repent, Jesus threatened to "remove their lampstand' which lampstands represent their right of being a church that belonged to Jesus. Two churches, Smyrna and Philadelphia, were *commended* by Jesus for their faithfulness.

Jesus' purpose in the letters was to challenge the churches to get their faith focused in the right place before the *impending crisis* which God warned would *soon* come upon them (Rev 1:1-3). An underlying message to all Christians and churches in all ages and situations is the need to develop a strong faith focused on Jesus and God before crises strike.

The danger confronting the churches was the temptation to compromise faith with the Roman Imperial Cult that would tempt the saints to worship the Emperor in addition to Jesus. In addition there was and is always the temptation out of convenience to compromise faith with the world of pagan unbelieving neighbors.

We will examine two letters in greater detail, the letter to Ephesus, which church needed repentance and renewed refocused love. The letter to Smyrna in which there is no condemnation, only encouragement, draws attention to the need to maintain a clear vision of faith. Time does not permit a full study of each of the letters, but similar themes run through each letter.

Several key theological points stand out clearly in the letters:

*First*, Jesus' awareness of what is going on in the life of each church. He knows their strengths as well as their weaknesses.

*Second*, Jesus does not overlook a lack of faith in his churches and calls churches to repent and return to a sincere faith.

*Third*, Jesus' promise to come *soon* to the unfaithful churches in judgment, *unless* they repent.

*Fourth*, Jesus' promise to reward those who remain faithful and conquer Satan through their uncompromising faith.

Jesus promises those who conquer (NIV, overcome) that is, who die as martyrs the reward of true spiritual food for eternal life and a throne and share in his reign and kingdom. Conquering in Revelation becomes a synonym for faithfulness to Jesus that results in martyrdom. The irony in Revelation is that by being conquered the saints will conquer Satan!

In each of the five letters of rebuke there is a call to repentance. Each letter will begin by identifying Jesus, the author of the letter, in terms of the magnificent powerful and conquering description of him in Rev 1:12-18. In each letter there is a section commending the church. There is also a section identifying their weakness and calling them to repentance. There is a reward promised for faithfully *conquering*. Finally, emphasizing the urgency of Jesus' message, each letter concludes with an encouragement to hear carefully Jesus' and the Holy Spirit's message.

## The Seven Churches of Asia (Rev 2, 3)

Two were faithful: Smyrna and Philadelphia. Five were unfaithful or had problems: Ephesus, Pergamum, Thyatira, Sardis, and Laodicea.

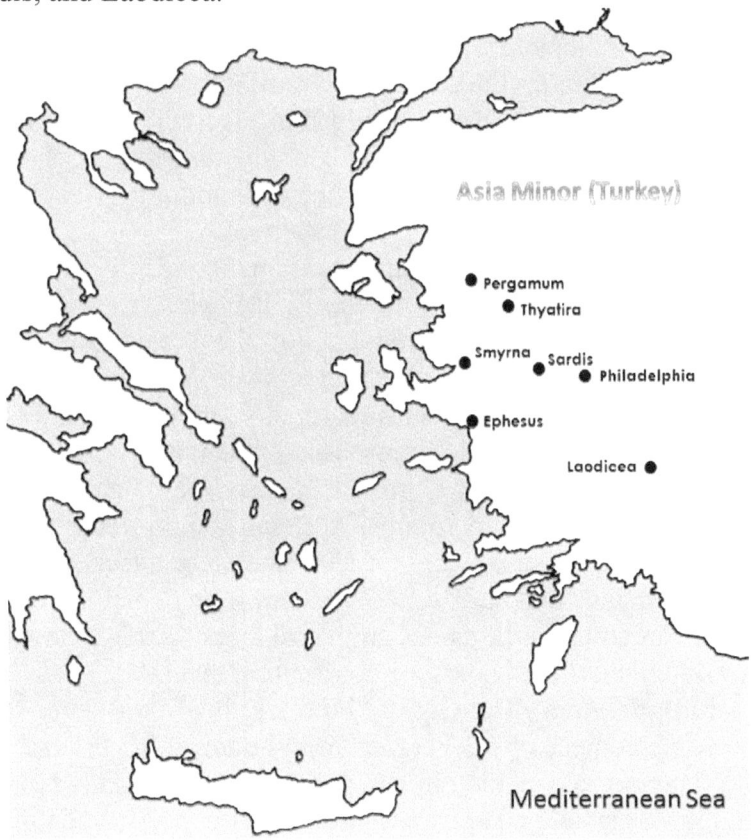

**Ephesus:** Ephesus was major sea port and a major religious center for Asia. The city had many Imperial Temples, one to Domitian. Perhaps the most significant influence beyond the Imperial Cult was the great Temple of the fertility goddess, Artemis. Paul and the Apostle John had spent many years teaching in Ephesus. Ephesus was most likely the springboard to missions in Asia.

**Smyrna:** This city was devoted to the Imperial Cult which obviously played a significant part in the persecution of the church. It was a major city in Asia. The Christians were most likely financially poor, and the Synagogue played a major role in their suffering and persecution.

**Pergamum:** Pergamum was the capital city of the Roman Province of Asia. It was dominated by the Imperial Cult and housed several important Imperial Temples as well as a major hospital, the Asklepion, and religio-medical shrine to the god of healing, Asklepios. The church was characterized by a compromised faith (the spirit of Balaam).

**Thyatira:** This was an industrial city with many smelting works as well as a source of the production of purple (Lydia, Acts 16:14). A Jezebel-like practice of immorality was tolerated by the church.

**Sardis:** Sardis had a long and fascinating history. In the past it had been the capital city of the Lydian king, Croesus who is famous for being considered one of the wealthiest kings of ancient times, the expression "rich as Croesus' exemplifies this! The city had an impregnable acropolis (mountain fortress) to which the Lydians would retreat when threatened. Legend has it that when threatened by Cyrus of Persia Croesus and his troops retreated into their acropolis. Being comfortable in their acropolis the Lydians were not alert and were attacked by night by the Persians and defeated. Jesus and John depict the problem in the church in Sardis as one similar to that of Croesus, not being awake and alert to the dangers confronting them.

**Philadelphia:** The city of "brotherly love" was so called by the King Eumenes II of Pergamum in honor of his brother. The City was a cross roads city on two major thoroughfares. The church was small and apparently opposed by the Synagogue.

**Laodicea:** Laodicea was a wealthy city and a major business center in Asia. A manufacturing hospital renowned for its eye salve was part of the city economy. The city did not maintain a military force, relying on its wealth to take care of its problems. The church took on the economic nature of the city and was self-reliant, not seeking any help, even divine help.

# A Detailed Look at Two Churches

We will look a little closer at two churches: one with problems, Ephesus; one faithful, Smyrna.

**Ephesus (Rev 2:1-7):**

Ephesus was a major seaport, and the cultural and religious center, of the Roman Province of Asia. The city was dominated by the magnificent Temple of Artemis, the fertility goddess of the region. A major theater and agora (market place) dominated the center of the city. By the time John wrote Revelation the two major streets of the city were lined with temples erected to the Roman Emperors with one to the emperor Domitian in which an enormous image of the emperor held a place of honor in the city. The Ephesian church was possibly the major center of Christianity in Asia (cf. Acts 19:26). The Ephesian church is one of five who receive condemnation and warning from Jesus with a call to repentance.

Rev 2:2, 3. The church was hard working, committed to church work and doctrinally sound, yet Jesus found the Ephesian Christians lacking in that they were motivated by the normal trappings of churches by seriously lacking in love. Jesus spoke firmly against this and called on the Ephesians to return to the love they had at first, that is, love for Jesus and one another Rev 2:2-4.

Rev 2:4-6. Jesus warned them that unless they repented he would come to them and judge them, taking their lampstand away, that is, take away their right to be His church. He told them he despised the Nicolaitans, apparently a licentious group who tolerated immorality, but commended the church for their hatred of this group's works.

Rev 2:7. We are introduced here to a theme that John will repeat in each letter. Those who *conquer* (NIV *overcome*) will be rewarded. We will learn that in Revelation *conquering* is a synonym for *dying as a martyr*. By dying faithfully to Jesus as a martyr the saints would *conquer* or overcome their oppressors and Satan who lay behind them. By conquering their enemies (in Revelation, Rome and her allies) Jesus would give the martyrs *the tree of life to eat*, meaning that they would live forever. The *tree of life* image draws on the tree in the Garden of Eden, Gen 2:9, of which God had told Adam and Eve that they could eat. In the Genesis story the tree of life is a symbol of real spiritual food that sustains life. The point here is that by dying faithfully Jesus would give them food for eternal life, and they would live again. The image of resurrection by the power of God is a powerful symbol in Revelation, especially for those who were being called on to die for their faith.

### Smyrna (Rev 2:8-11):

Two out of the seven churches in Revelation receive no condemnation from Jesus. They are Smyrna and Philadelphia. For several reasons this church and letter are special! First, Smyrna was an important city, a major seaport, and a city faithful to the goddess Roma (representing the Imperial Cult). Smyrna was attributed by the ancient historians as possibly the most beautiful city in the Roman Empire. Even today, Izmir, as it is now known, remains a beautiful city lying between the sea and mountains. It is a major city in the nation of Turkey. The modern population is well over 3 million.

Church history identifies Smyrna as the home of one of the early faithful bishops of the church, Polycarp, who died as a martyr following betrayal by the Synagogue. Eusebius in his *Ecclesiastical History*, Book III, xv records that the Roman governor, after trying to get Polycarp to offer incense to the Emperor Domitian, ordered Polycarp to be put to death in the Agora (market place). The governor "pressed Polycarp" saying "Take the oath and I will let you go, revile Christ". Polycarp's response to the governor was "For eighty and six years have I been his servant, and he has done me no wrong, and how can I blaspheme my King who saved me? ... If you vainly suppose that I will swear by the genius of Caesar, as you say, and pretend that you are ignorant who I am, listen plainly: I am a Christian..."

Jesus acknowledged the Smyrnaean's tribulation (persecution and suffering) and reinforced that part of their problem was the Jewish Synagogue which he identified as a synagogue of Satan (Rev 2:9). Obviously the synagogue was partially responsible for their suffering and persecution. As we noticed in the case of

Polycarp, this was still the situation some 60 years after Revelation was written.

Rev 2:10. Jesus' promise to the Smyrnaen Christians for conquering was that they would receive a *crown of life* (the Greek word for *crown* is *stephanos*, meaning the victory *laurel* wreath representing victory in the athletic games. This is not a royal crown, *diadēma*, but a *victor's* wreath.) The actual reward symbolized by the crown was as in Rev 2:7, life! The conquering martyr would not be hurt by the second death, that is, the final judgment (Rev 20:14).

## A Survey of Jesus' Call to Repentance and Rewards Promised to the Seven Churches for Conquering or Dying as Martyrs

**Ephesus** – repent and return to the love they had at first. For conquering they would receive the tree of life; the conquering martyr would live forever (Rev 2:7).

**Smyrna** – faithful, promised the crown (laurel wreath of victory) of life; they would not be hurt by the second death, the final judgment (Rev 2:10, 11).

**Pergamum** – threatened by the Imperial Cult and tolerant of a compromised faith (the spirit of Balaam). The faithful were promised hidden manna for conquering, that is, spiritual food that sustains life. They were also promised a small white stone, symbolic of an invitation to the great heavenly eschatological banquet at the end of time (Rev 2:17).

**Thyatira** – threatened by a Jezebel spirit of immorality. The conquerors were promised power over the nations, and a rod of iron like Jesus had received (Psalm 2, the psalm of kingly ascent) to rule over the nations (Rev 2:27, 28). The conquering martyrs will reign with Jesus in his kingdom.

**Sardis** – they were comfortable, asleep, and uncommitted. The conquerors were promised white garments which symbolized faithfulness and victory; their names would not be blotted out of the book of life (Rev 3:5).

**Philadelphia** – this church was faithful. The conquerors would become pillars in the temple of God (Rev 12).

**Laodicea** – a wealthy and self-reliant city and church. The conquerors were promised that they would sit with Jesus on his throne (Rev 3:21).

## The Rewards of an Uncompromising Faithfulness to Jesus

This is a survey of the rewards of an uncompromising faithfulness to Jesus. The promises to the seven churches are as relevant today as they were 2000 years ago! Conquering saints, those who are willing to give their lives for Jesus, are given a victory crown (laurel wreath of victory). Seemingly defeated by Satan and Rome in this life, they in fact are the ultimate conquerors who reign with Jesus on his throne. Sometimes life is difficult and the price almost too heavy to bear! However, the rewards far outweigh the cost, as Paul observed (Rom 8:18) "I consider that the sufferings of this present time are not worth comparing with the glory that is to be revealed to us."

Remember Rom 8:37ff, *Christians are more than conquerors through him who loved us*. Those who conquer are given spiritual food which sustains them for eternal life. They sit on thrones and reign with Christ in his kingdom. Christians should seek such food for eternal life while they can!

Those who conquer sit with Jesus on his throne and reign completely with him in his kingdom. They have no part in the Roman kingdom but share in Jesus' kingdom. Primarily this means that Jesus is their sovereign Lord and they enjoy all of the eternal benefits from this.

Those who conquer may have their name erased from the Roman citizenship list, but they will have their name written in the Lamb's book of life. Their name will not be blotted out of the book of life. The world may reject Christians but Jesus and God will not.

Those who conquer and are willing to give their lives to Jesus have an invitation from Jesus to God's final great eschatological banquet in heaven. The Lord's Supper is an advanced (proleptic) experience of this end time spiritual feast that waits for us in heaven.

## Lessons We Learn from this Chapter and the Seven Letters

- Christians and churches must examine their faith to determine whether they have their faith focused in the right place, that is, in Jesus.
- Jesus is well aware of our faith, our strengths and weaknesses, and will judge us for a compromised faith.
- Our present day decisions have end of the world implications and consequences.
- Jesus had taught that his disciples cannot serve two masters. Service to the world and service to Jesus cannot take place at the same time.
- Christians must decide who they will serve!
- Without realizing it, like the Laodiceans, Christians today control their own lives and do not understand what living in the kingdom of Jesus really means. We too often rely on our own strength or ability not realizing that we desperately need God, Jesus, and the Holy Spirit in our lives.
- The following Scriptures illustrate this well, Joshua 24:14-15, "choose this day whom you will serve whether the gods your fathers served…but for me and my house, we will serve the Lord."
- Matt 6:24, "No one can serve two masters; for either he will hate the one and love the other, or he will be devoted to the one and despise the other."
- God challenges each one of us to examine our faith, refocus our faith, and commit to an uncompromising faith in and love for Jesus.
- Church is important, hard work is important, sound doctrine is important, but it is an uncompromising faith in, and love for, Jesus that God is looking for.

## Our Next Chapter

Rev 4 is really where the mystical visions of Revelation begin. To set the scene John takes us on a mystical journey right into the throne room of God where we "see" God in all of his holiness and glory. Rev 5-8 introduces God holding a scroll that only Jesus is able to reveal. This scroll represents God's plan for dealing with the problem of evil. Jesus is the center of God's plan.

# Chapter 6
# The Throne Room and Scroll:
# Revelation 4; 5:1-8:5

## Introduction

The Heavenly Throne Room and Scroll are vital to understanding the theme and message of Revelation. Although these chapters cover a great amount of material we will focus on the major themes of the book.

As before, we will note that John draws extensively from the Old Testament, the Jewish/Christian Apocalyptic Tradition, the Apocrypha, and the Pseudepigrapha to paint impressionistic pictures of the dramatic cosmic scenes and visions of Revelation.

## Rev 4 – The Heavenly Throne Room

This chapter reveals a scene that is vital to both John's and the churches' ability to understand the serious challenge God is about to make to the Churches in Asia. God is going to ask the saints to be willing to give their lives as a sacrifice to Jesus. He will ask the martyred saints to be patient while he works his plan of redemption (*Heilsgeschichte*) which will involve oppression and suffering from an evil world. It is important for both John and the churches to catch a glimpse of God in all of his Holiness, Sovereignty, Righteousness, and Glory so they can see the larger picture of God's plan and not be focused on their own situation as serious as it may be.

## Rev 5 – The Scroll

Chapter 5 is a continuation of the Heavenly Throne Room scene with God on his throne holding a large scroll in his right hand. Scrolls play an important role in the Jewish apocalyptic and literary tradition. Scrolls signify that God has a plan that he is working. Sometimes the plan involves the future, at other times it involves the immediate future. The sealing of a scroll implies a plan for the future, the breaking of seals or not sealing a scroll implies a plan for the immediate future. This scroll explains that God has a plan and that he is working his plan. This scroll speaks of God's plan for dealing with the problem of evil. In the case of the churches in Asia in the first century God wants the churches to see that their circumstances are part of that plan and that God would in his time take care of their situation. In the interim he encourages them to remain faithful and promises them that he will ensure their future and vindicate their present. We should remember that the genius of apocalyptic is to be pessimistic about the potential of human ability and history to solve problems, and optimistic about God's divine intervention and ability to take care of their future. This scroll will explain that God can and does use evil to serve his purpose of getting evil men to see their failure and repent.

## Rev 6 – The Seven Seals

Only Jesus is able to break open the seven seals on the great scroll indicating that Jesus has a major role to play in God's *Heilsgeschichte* or plan for saving his world, including the saints. The first four seals involve the *four living creatures* whose responsibility it is to proclaim and defend God's holiness. Four horsemen ride onto the scene. In the tradition of Zechariah their duty is to serve God and proclaim his purpose. Six extraordinary seals are opened revealing striking scenes and images. Each of these scenes and events is under the power and authority of God and explain how he uses various events and circumstances to achieve his purpose. The seven seals also explain the sovereignty of God over all things. When the story reaches toward the climax of the seventh seal John inserts the first of several interludes which are intended to slow things down while God continues his story. The sixth seal reveals signs of apocalyptic judgments that are truly earth and heaven shaking! Such apocalyptic signs in the Old and new Testaments are related to and express God's judgments on rebellious nations that oppose his people and purpose. Before the final seal is opened things must be carefully considered, so we have the first interlude of Rev 7.

## Rev 7 – The Interlude

The Interlude of chapter seven reveals two scenes. Both are like the story of Revelation highly symbolic. The first is the sealing of God's people. Sealing implies ownership and protection. The symbolic 144,000 is understood to represent the church militant. The second is of a great multitude standing before God's throne. This multitude is understood to be symbol of the church victorious. The purpose of this Interlude is to reassure the saints that although they are in a war and many will die, they will be victorious. Their presence in the throne room with the Lamb assures them of this.

## The Heavenly Throne Room (Rev 4)

In the manner of the prophets Isaiah and Ezekiel John is "transported" in a vision into heaven to the throne room of God. John is tapping into the Jewish mystical "chariot scene" tradition drawn from Enoch's experience of being transported into the presence of God. Such mystical experiences were understood to give the "prophet" insight into the mysteries of God that otherwise would or could not be known.

The throne room in Rev 4 is like a war command center. We are reminded of Adela Yarbro Collins' observation that we should interpret Revelation in the context of Combat Mythology. God directs the action of war and judgment and his vindication of the saints out of this heavenly throne room. The throne room reminds us that God is the ultimate controller of all things in heaven and on earth.

In the throne room there is a sea, glasslike like crystal. In Revelation the sea represents a major source of evil (cf. Rev 13 where an evil beast comes out of the sea, and Rev 21:1, where after Satan is judged the sea is no more). In the throne room evil is "tamed" or "controlled" by the presence of God and his holiness. In the presence of God's holiness, evil (Rome and Satan) is shown to be no real threat to the power of God and ultimately under God's control. This is important to the message of Revelation and the argument that evil in the presence of God's righteousness amounts to nothing. We call this kind of argument a theodicy which is a defense of God's power, righteousness, and sovereignty in the presence of threatening evil.

Also in the throne room are four living creatures (cf. Ezekiel 1). They always represent the holiness of God, they symbolize that holiness, protect God's holiness, and sing of his glory and holiness. In Rev 4 as elsewhere they sing a hymn to the holiness of God. They are joined by 24 elders in that hymn. The twenty four elders represent the martyrs of all time (12 OT and 12 NT) and are symbolic of the 24 priestly orders of the Mosaic system. The elders throw their crowns (*stephanoi*, laurel wreaths of victory) before the throne of God, indicating that they see their martyrdom as a sacrifice to God. (Remember at Rev 2:10 that conquerors or martyrs in Revelation received such victory crowns). Uppermost in this heavenly scene are the *holiness* and *sovereignty* of God. John and the churches in Asia (as do all Christians) need to see and understand the majesty, holiness, and sovereignty of God.

## The Scroll (Rev 5)

In this chapter we are still in the heavenly throne room of God who is seated on his throne with a scroll in his right hand. In the Jewish and Pseudepigraphical tradition scrolls represent the fact that God has a plan of how he intends to take care of a situation (Dan 12:4; Ezek 2:9, 10; Isa 29:11; Odes Solomon 33:8; et al). In this case it will reveal God's plan for dealing with the problem of evil, specifically the problem the church is facing with Roman oppression. This heavenly scroll is sealed by seven seals indicating that it is completely sealed and can only be opened or understood by the intervention of Jesus.

In apocalyptic terms we might call this scroll God's ultimate plan of redemption for all of creation for God is not only concerned for an immediate problem but is also concerned for the big picture of evil.

No one is able to open the seals of the scroll except Jesus. This focuses attention on the fact that Jesus is the only one who is able to open the scroll and reveal its message. It also reveals the fact that Jesus holds the answer to, the solution of the problem of evil.

Jesus is worthy to open the scroll and reveal its message because he "was slain and by his blood ransomed men for God" (Rev 5:9). Jesus' death and resurrection (a prototype of Christian martyrdom) is God's answer to the problem of evil. Jesus' death and resurrection is symbolic of his victory and power over the power of Satan and evil. (Cf. Rev 12:10, 11.)

An interesting collage of thought is presented in the messianic statement regarding Jesus. He is in one breath the Lion of the tribe of Judah, the root of David, and in the next breath he is a lamb! The connection of a sacrificial lamb and messianic ruling is interesting and foundational to the message of Revelation. Jesus reigned by dying on a cross. The martyrs will reign with him by offering their lives to him as a sacrifice!

All of heaven focuses now on Jesus and worships him in hymns of praise and glory! Jesus becomes the central theme of the message of Revelation!

John introduces an interesting and important point at Rev 5:8, the prayers of the saints. We will see at Rev 6:10ff that this prayer was a prayer for vindication for their suffering and death. John will pick this thought up at Rev 6:10, 8:3, 4, and 10:6 as he builds his story of God's concern for the saints.

## The Seven Seals (Rev 6; 8:1-5)

The scroll in God's hand that Jesus takes and begins to open emphasizes that God has a plan for dealing with the problem of evil. The seven seals explain that God can and does use evil and evil men to achieve his purpose. The seven seals move the reader progressively toward the seventh seal which should bring down the curtain of the drama that John is unfolding. However, when we get to that point we will be taken into seven trumpets of divine warning judgments that are intended to bring evil men to repentance. This gracious gift they refuse but God does not give up that easily. He persists and John carries us on through seven plagues reminiscent of the plagues of Egypt and God's judgment on an evil nation.

Several salient points need to be mentioned here. *First*, the progress through the seals to the trumpets and then on through the plagues need to be understood as developing acts within the drama introduced by the scroll in God's hands. The story of the scroll continues throughout Revelation. The seals, trumpets, plagues, etc. are all part of the mystery being revealed by Jesus in the scroll. *Second*, the developing scenes should not be seen as sequential acts in a time line. They are better understood as kaleidoscopic views of the story in a repetitive progression as in Hendriksen's progressive parallelism (see the discussion of this in the Chapter 3, John's Literary Genius). It might help to refer to the structure for Revelation described in chapter 3 of this study. The Greek syntax that connects the various seals and scenes makes it clear that the scenes are not sequential but are repetitive. *Third*, the scenes introduced in the seven seals and later scenes are drawn from images from the Jewish literary tradition whose symbolism the readers and audience would understand. Our challenge is to see the symbolism and endeavor to not interpret them literally.

## The Seven Seals

The first four seals are introduced with a link to the four living creatures of Rev 4 whose task it was to proclaim and defend the holiness of God. That the four horsemen in Rev 6:1ff are sent out, even commissioned by the four living creatures are intended to demonstrate that they act within the holiness and sovereignty of God. Six seals are opened in this section with the seventh following an Interlude in Rev 7. The six seals reveal a series of catastrophes and judgments. That they are part of the scroll demonstrates that they fall within the *"Heilsgeschichen"* plan of redemption of God. The seventh seal follows the Interlude of Rev 7 and "morphs" into seven trumpets in Rev 8.

**War – Rev 6:1-2:** The first horseman on a white horse represents war. Our knowledge of the Old Testament should inform us that God has used war as a means of getting the attention of evil men and to achieve his purpose. God's purpose of drawing attention to war was to remind the Christians that God is supreme even over war. His power transcends even that of war. Although we today dislike war we still can recognize that sometimes war has been used to remove an evil nation or power.

**Rebellion – Rev 6:3-4:** The second horseman on a red horse represents rebellion. God has used rebellions to challenge powerful nations. The constant threat of rebellions kept Rome "humble"! The enormous power of Rome was constantly threatened by uprisings among its vast empire. Consider the Jewish rebellion at Masada ca. A.D. 72/73. The powerful Roman army was engaged with some 960 zealots at this mountain fortress for over two years before they eventually took the stronghold.

**Famine – Rev 6:5-6:** Famine was a constant issue for Rome, especially in areas that had been impoverished by war and Rome's scorched earth policy. Providing food within its far flung borders was a constant problem to Rome. This third horseman on a black horse obviously represents famine and is intended to remind Rome of its interior weakness.

**Death – Rev 6:7-8:** Although Rome believed it held the key to life and death; even they knew that death lay beyond their control. Old Testament stories remind us that God has and can use the death of a king to achieve his purpose. Likewise every Roman Emperor was aware of threats to his own life. Eight of the first eleven emperors from Augustus to Domitian were murdered, assassinated, or committed suicide. Even emperors could not escape death!

**Martyrdom – Rev 6:9-11:** The fifth seal opened is not introduced by a horseman but its relevance to the churches in Asia would not be lost on Revelation's readers. This seal and its events become a repeated theme throughout Revelation. We will encounter here one of John's significant *rebirth of images* initiatives in Revelation. John strategically introduces a new thought and then comes back to it on several occasions as he builds on this message. Here we encounter souls that have been slain (martyrs) beneath an altar crying out in prayer to God. Their cry or prayer to God is for vindication, *"How long before you judge and avenge our blood upon those who dwell on the earth?" First* we notice that they are given *white robes.* White robes in the combat genre of Revelation are symbols of victory. *Second* the slain saints are crying out not simply for vengeance but for the vindication of their death. They need to know that their death had a significant meaning in God's scheme of things. *Third*, we encounter a puzzling thought that God has in mind a specific number of people who must die before he does anything! However, those familiar with the apocalyptic genre and literature would know that this is a symbol for God being aware of what is happening to his people. *Fourth*, John speaks of those *who dwell on the earth.* This sounds like everyone who lives on the earth. However, again in the apocalyptic tradition the readers would know that this image refers to those whose life center is earthly and not heavenly. In Revelation John will, in an interesting display of a rebirth of images, explain progressively through his story that those who dwell on the earth are those who worship the beast and bear the number of the beast (666, a man's number or human number).

**Apocalyptic Signs – Rev 6:12-17:** The sixth seal reveals an array of dramatic apocalyptic signs. This genre would have been clearly understood by those who knew their Old Testament and apocalyptic literature. This language was used on several occasions in the Old Testament in contexts where God judges an evil nation for oppressing his people or opposing his purpose. Cf. Isa 13:9-11, God's judgment on Babylon; Isa 24:21-23, God's judgment on sinful nations; Isa 34:1-4, God's judgment on the nations; Ezek 32:7, 8, God's judgment on Egypt; Joel 2:30-32, God's judgment on Zion and Jerusalem. Similar language is used by Matthew describing the judgment of Jerusalem, Matt 24:28. Apocalyptic upheavals and cosmic catastrophes were not accounts of natural catastrophes but symbols of God's divine judgments. The "catastrophic events" are not understood as literal events but are symbolically interpreted as "signs" of God's divine intervention. Only God has the power to bring about such "events"! These apocalyptic signs in Rev 6:12ff remind the

Christians that God will in his time and according to his purpose take care of Rome!

**The Seventh Seal - Seven Trumpets of Judgment (Rev 8:1-5):** We expect following the sixth seal to encounter the seventh seal being opened. However, before this tales place John inserts an Interlude to slow things down and assure the saints that they are not overlooked by God, but have already been sealed by God which symbolizes being owned and protected by God. We will examine this Interlude below. John will bring us back to the seventh seal at Rev 8:1-6 where he will introduce seven trumpets. In his unique literary style of connecting or linking his scenes the seventh seal becomes seven trumpets.

**The importance of Rev 6:10.** In the fifth seal we saw the saints crying out to God for vindication and judgment on their enemy. "How long before you judge…" They are told to wait while God works his plan. The lesson to be learned from this to be patient while God works his plan of salvation in human experience (cf. 2 Pet 3:8-10). His plan includes the opportunity for even evil men to come to repentance. John will return to this prayer on several occasions such as Rev 8:3, 4 and 10:6 as he links the events being discussed back to the prayers of the saints.

## The Interlude of Rev 7: the 144,000 and a Great Multitude

This text has been seriously misused by literalists such as the Jehovah Witnesses. The number 144,000 and twelve tribes of Israel are obviously symbolic, as are all the numbers in Revelation and the apocalyptic genre. A careful examination of the twelve tribes of Israel reveals that this list is not precise! For instance, Judah is mentioned first which is not traditional, Dan is not included, and Joseph and Manasseh are included as tribes. There is no mention of Ephraim. John is obviously using the tribes stylishly to symbolize God's people and not simply the twelve tribes of Israel. The numbering of the people is drawn from numbering an army or group involved in a military campaign. The 144,000 represent God's church militant (cf. Rev 14:1-5 in which vss. 4,5 are military symbols drawn from the OT,

1 Sam 21:4,5; Deut 20; Deut 23:9,10). The number 144,000 informs the careful reader that the church is in a war. At this point the enemy has not been specified, but by the time we reach Rev 12, 13, and 14 we realize that the enemy is Rome as an agent of Satan.

The 144,000 are sealed by God, symbols of His *ownership* and *protection*. They might die for their faith, but death is not ultimate. They are raised to reign with the Lamb (cf. Rev 2 and 3 and the reward of the martyrs). The second part of the Interlude identifies a great multitude and reveals who they are. These are the souls that have died for their faith and are now in the throne room with the Lamb. As conquerors they have been robed in white robes (victory). Together with the four living creatures and the elders they sing a hymn of praise to God, Salvation (victory) belongs to our God who sits on the throne and to the Lamb." The saints have become conquerors through their death and resurrection and now reign with Jesus.

In this Interlude we see the church militant (the 144,000) and the church victorious (the great multitude before God's throne in heaven

## The Seventh Seal and Seven Trumpets (Rev 8:1-5)

The seventh seal is so important that there is silence in heaven for 30 minutes before it is opened! We are introduced here to one of John's unique literary techniques, the linking of one series of vision to the next. The intention is not to explain a sequential series of visions but one of a repetition or enlargement of the story John is revealing. The seventh seal "morphs" into seven warning trumpets of God's judgment. The images revealed in the seven trumpets draw on Israel's exodus experience in Egypt during the plagues, and other apocalyptic images. We will learn in the next chapter that these are warning judgments on Rome calling them to repentance. They are not images of the final end of the world judgment.

## Lessons to learn from this Chapter and the Seven Seals

- We have already learned that God is in control of everything, even evil. The sea in the throne room was calm and not threatening in the presence of the Almighty God. The throne room scene reveals that God is sovereign ruler of heaven and earth.
- The scroll in God's hand reveals that God has a plan (*Heilsgeschichte*) for dealing with the problem of evil, and that plan centers on Jesus and his death and resurrection.
- The seals reveal that God can and does use evil and evil men to achieve his purpose of redemption. He sends warning judgments on evil men to bring them to repentance.
- Faith (trusting) in God and the power of Jesus' death and resurrection is the solution to the problem of evil and suffering. Through an uncompromising faith in Jesus, God guarantees Christians victory over evil.
- God has promised that should Christians die for that faith then He will raise them to the eternal kingdom where they will reign with Jesus (cf. Rom 8:11).
- All this is made possible by Jesus' victory over Satan in his death and resurrection.
- Although the martyrs die for their faith, they are protected (sealed) by God. They may die for their faith, but God will save them eternally in heaven where they will celebrate their victory over Satan.
- A major point made in this section (Rev 6:10) is that Christians must be patient while God works his plan.

## Our Next Chapter

In this chapter we will examine The Seven Warning Trumpets (Rev 8, 9). We will notice that these trumpets are warning trumpets calling on evil men to repent and worship God.

They refuse so John progresses to finalize the seven trumpets at Rev 10, 11.

# Chapter 7

# The Seven Warning Trumpets: Revelation 8 & 9

## Introduction

We need to remember that this section of Revelation on the Seven Trumpets is still part of the scroll of Rev 5 which represents God's plan for dealing with the problem of evil and suffering, and is in fact an extension of the seventh seal of Rev 6:1-8:5. The seven trumpets about to be blown are so important that heaven comes to a standstill and is silent while the seventh seal is opened (Rev 8:1). We learn from Rev 9:20 that these seven trumpets of God's judgment are not total judgments, or the final end of the world judgment, but are warning trumpets calling on the enemies of the saints to repent, which they refuse to do.

The first three trumpets reveal plagues poured out on the earth, but their judgment is only partial (only 1/3 of the trees, sea, and waters suffer) – the image draws on the Egypt/Exodus typology. John expects the readers to recall the 10 plagues on Egypt prior to the Exodus (why seven plagues in Revelation not 10 as in Exodus 7ff? This is Revelation and things get done in sevens!).

The fourth and fifth trumpets are set in apocalyptic and cosmic visions. The seventh is interesting and in fact introduces a triumphant concept of judgment. Toward the close of the seven warning trumpets, between the sixth and seventh trumpet, there is another Interlude; Rev 10 and 11:1-14. We will examine this Interlude in the next chapter.

Notice how John connects this section to the prayers of the saints for vindication at Rev 6:10 (Rev 8:3 speaks of the prayers of the saints). At Rev 6:10 the saints were told to wait while God worked his plan of redemption. This section regarding the 7 trumpets explains that God is working his plan. His plan involves calling on evil men to repent before he finally brings judgment on them. This reminds us that although God is a holy and sovereign God he is also a righteous God who gives all men the opportunity to repent.

## The First Three Warning Trumpets
## (Rev 8:7-11)

These three trumpets are shaped by the Mosaic Egypt plagues. We gather from this analogy that these trumpets are warning trumpets as were the plagues on Egypt plagues. The symbols John builds into these trumpets would have been familiar to Christians living in the Roman world at the close of the first century AD who knew the recent history of Rome as well as their Old Testament and apocalyptic literature.

**Rev 8:7. The First Warning Trumpet.** Although the events of this trumpet would call to mind the Egyptian plagues, their apocalyptic relationship would have been well known to the readers of Revelation. We are introduced here to an interesting feature of apocalyptic judgments; they are often poured out on the physical world rather than on mankind! Note Rom 8:18ff. It is the physical world that mourns over man's sins and awaits eagerly the revelation of the sons of God. Rom 8:18ff is steeped in the apocalyptic genre. That only one third of the physical world is impacted informs us that the judgment is a warning judgment and not a total judgment.

**Rev 8:8, 9. The Second Warning Trumpet.** The great mountain falling into the sea may be a reminder of Mt Vesuvius (a volcano) and the city of Pompey. Vesuvius erupted in A.D. 79 and destroyed Pompey, a Roman sea resort. We learn from *the Sibylline Oracles* (apocalyptic literature dated ca. 150 B.C. to fifth century A.D.) that the Jews and Christians interpreted the eruption of Mt. Vesuvius at Pompey as God's judgment on Rome.

**Rev 8:10, 11. The Third Trumpet.** The star falling from heaven reminded the Christians of the king of Babylon being judged by God in Isa 14:12ff for his oppression of Israel. The symbolism now points to the Emperor of Rome as the fallen star! Babylon will feature prominently later in Revelation as a symbol for Rome. In the first six centuries of Christianity every reference to Babylon is in the context of Rome. Again only one third of the physical world is judged.

## The Fourth Trumpet (Rev 8:12, 13)

Once again John describes a judgment in term of the apocalyptic genre of cosmic catastrophes, this time however, it is only a third of the constellations and sky that are impacted. The message is still the same, God is making a statement to the churches that unless Rome repents he will judge them in the same manner he has judged evil nations in the past. An additional note is included in this fourth trumpet; an eagle appears in mid-heaven (the sky) crying three woes. *First*, woes are traditionally apocalyptic signs of judgments. Cf. Matt 23 where Jesus pronounces seven woes on Jerusalem and the religious leaders of the synagogue. *Second*, the word translated eagle in our better translations is *aetos*, a large bird of carrion, eagle, or vulture. It might be better to translate this bird as a vulture. Vultures are associated with death and this bird is proclaiming apocalyptic woes which are associated with death!

## The Final Three Warning Trumpets (Rev 9:1-21 and 11:15-19)

The fifth and sixth warning trumpets are "demonic" warnings; the seventh and last trumpet represents a "triumphant" announcement.

**The Fifth Trumpet.** This trumpet announces a swarm of locusts that come from the bottomless pit, one of the Jewish symbols of the source of evil. The locust figure is drawn from Joel 2 where locusts were a symbol of God's judgment on Jerusalem and Judah. The locusts are reminiscent of sinister armies (the Parthians) that were a constant threat to Rome. The warning "statements" which carry a Persian image would have been understood by persons living in the eastern corridor of the Roman Empire. Persia was the one nation and world power that Rome had not been able to conquer and which remained a constant threat to Rome. The interesting play on names at the end of this trumpet scene draws the attention of the reader back to Rome. The Hebrew *Abaddon* is paralleled to the Greek *Apollyon, the destroyer*. God would bring the mythical *destroyer*, in this context Persia and the Parthian army, against Rome!

**The Sixth Trumpet.** This one is also reminiscent of the fearful Parthian army. Locating this army at the Euphrates River clarifies who it is that John is describing. The fact that he refers to cavalry focuses on the Parthians since the Roman army were foot soldiers. The fearsome nature of these soldiers is intended to drive home the seriousness of God's warning judgment on Rome. The paragraph of Rev 9:20ff highlights God's purpose in sending these warning judgments on Rome. *Repentance*! This is a reminder to the saints and all readers that God is a righteous God who gives all men every opportunity to repent. The plagues of these warning trumpets were intended to bring Rome and the oppressors of the saints to repentance, but they would not give up worshipping demons and idols of gold and silver (presumably the Imperial Cult and emperor worship). Nor did they give up their murders!

## The Interlude and Seventh Trumpet (Rev 10:1-11:14 and 11:15-19)

Before we get to the seventh climactic and "triumphant" trumpet John introduces another interlude (Rev 10 - Rev 11:14). This interlude discusses the eating of a little scroll (drawn from Ezek 2:8-3:3) and the measuring of the temple which symbolizes the protection of the saints (cf. Rev 11:1-14). This Interlude slows things down again and explains that the saints are in fact sealed and protected by God. They will suffer and many would die as martyrs, but ultimately they will be victorious through Jesus. This Interlude is important to the theology of Revelation and we will examine it in the next lesson.

The final seventh trumpet reveals the saints and all heaven rejoicing that God has taken up and demonstrated his reign over all the earth. We should not project this scene into a temporal context but see it in its intended symbolism. The implication is that God has judged the enemies of the saints. This reminds us that it is God, not Satan or Rome who is in control of all creation and the earth.

## Lessons We Learn from the Chapter and the Sixth Trumpets

- As God has warned the saints of the impending suffering and persecution, now He warns those oppressing the saints of his sure judgment.
- This is intended to encourage the saints that God has not forgotten them! The seven trumpets represent warning trumpets in which God calls on evil men to repent (Cf. Rev 9:20, 21).
- If they do not repent, then he will execute his judgment and sovereign reign over all creation, in apocalyptic symbolism, over those who persecute the saints.
- The seven trumpets are also a warning to the saints not to compromise their faith in Jesus and be caught up in the idolatry and immorality of the Imperial Cult.
- The saints needed assurance that God would vindicate them.
- In this section we learn that God is working on his plan.
- At the seventh trumpet we will see all heaven rejoicing in that they see God finally executing his plan and his sovereign reign.
- The reader must be careful not to project these trumpet messages into a temporal timeline of history but must see them as a symbolic scene in a theological drama. The question should not be when does this take place (a temporal context) but what does it mean (a symbolic context).
- The message is that Christians must wait patiently while God gives all men time and opportunity to repent (cf. 2 Pet 3:8-10).

- He will in his purpose and time take care of the situation. It is in this symbolic message that apocalyptic genre seeks to call believers to faith.
- In the section covered in Rev 12-Rev 20 John will describe these scenes in more specific detail. We will see John retelling the story, or preaching again in greater specificity (cf. Rev 10:11).

## Our Next Chapter

Chapter 8 will cover the Interlude of Rev 10-11:14 and the Seventh Trumpet of Rev 11:15-19. This chapter highlights two significant themes. *First*, God has heard the cry of the saints under the altar and will respond to it in due course. *Second*, when he finally does bring judgment on Rome and the enemies of the church the scene is one of triumphant celebration that God has taken up his sovereign power and is reigning over all creation.

# Chapter 8

# The Second Interlude and Seventh Trumpet: Revelation 10 & 11

## Introduction

Following Rev 6:17 when the sixth seal had been opened at a point of traumatic impact, John slowed things down in order to reassure the saints that they need have no fear of the severe judgment about to be poured out on "those who dwell on the earth" (that is, those who worship the beast, receive its mark, and oppress the saints (cf. Rev 6:10; 13:8, 14). At Rev 6:10 the martyred saints "beneath the alter" had cried out for vindication. They had been told to wait a little longer while God worked his plan and purpose. At a strategic point John introduced his first Interlude, Rev 7.

Now following the sixth warning trumpet John introduces another similar Interlude with the intention of explaining what was about to take place was an answer to the prayers of the saints. There would be no more delay (Rev 10:6). They need not fear the impending wrath of God and his judgments (cf. Rev 6:10, 8:5; 10:6). At Rev 11:1ff they would be "measured" as a sign that God knew all about them and had protected them.

The seven warning trumpets we have just studied are connected to this prayer for vindication (cf. Rev 8:5). Now in this second Interlude the saints will be assured that there would be no more delay (Rev 10:6) in response to their prayer for vindication. Rev 9:20, 21 at the conclusion of the sixth warning trumpet introduced a call for evil men to repent. This was an important concept in explaining the "delay" in God's response to the prayers of the saints at Rev 6:10. God wanted all men to have an opportunity to repent. Now he was ready to move on with his plan. Six trumpets have sounded and the readers wait in eager anticipation for the seventh trumpet, but before it is sounded they needed to hear another Interlude of explanation.

The first part of the Interlude, Rev 10, is not difficult to follow. The second part, Rev 11, opens with a difficult section but moves on to reassure the saints that even if they die as faithful witnesses to Jesus they will be raised by the power of God to reign with Jesus.

## The Little Scroll of Rev 10

Ezekiel 2:8-3:3 and Ezekiel's instruction to eat a scroll and then preach God's message is important to understanding this Interlude. The "little scroll" of Rev 10:2ff is intended to be a "chapter" in the large scroll of Rev 5. It continues the story that God has a plan for redeeming his people and taking care of the problem of evil.

John was about to write down more of the message but was told to seal up the message and not write it down for there was to be "no more delay". This implies that God's judgment was both certain and imminent. We remember Daniel was told to seal up the scroll he had written for the message was not for his time (Dan 12:4). Now the time is ready, there was to be no more delay, and the message regarding God's imminent judgment on Rome was to be described.

A note of caution is necessary at this point! The reader is tempted to read this judgment into a temporal context and this is not John's intention. He is merely drawing attention to the fact that Rome in God's plan had already been judged! Rome would eventually be judged at the end of time along with all the ungodly, but God was now ready to pronounce that judgment on Rome ahead of the end time. In theological eschatological terms we call this a *proleptic eschatological announcement*! It is an announcement pronounced ahead of time.

Like Ezekiel, John was told to eat the little scroll and when he did he would find that the message would be "bitter to his stomach and sweet as honey in his mouth". His message had two sides to it! It was bitter in that the saints would have to die for their faith, but sweet in that God would raise them to sit with Jesus on his throne with victory laurels (crowns) on their heads (Rev 2, 3).

The message also like Ezekiel's informs John to prophesy again about many peoples, nations, tongues, and kings! In other words, there is still more to come in God's purpose and message (Rev 12-22). So, in spite of there being no more delay, the message of Revelation continues! John will tell the story he has been telling again in greater specificity and detail.

## Measuring the Temple and the Two Witnesses (Rev 11:1-3)

Rev 11:1-3 is one of the more difficult passages in Revelation to unravel. It obviously draws on Ezekiel 40:1-5 and the measuring of the rebuilt Temple after the Babylonian exile, and on Zech 2:1-5. Both of these passages speak of God's redemptive plan, the return of his holiness to his city now lying desolate from the plunder of Israel's enemies who had been God's servants of judgment on Israel for their rebellion. They also speak of persecution and God's protection of the inhabitants of the city, that is, the faithful remnant.

In addition to Zech 2 John also draws on Daniel 7:25 and 12:7ff which speak of three and one half times (3 ½ years) and forty two months. Demonstrating that he is using these "temporal signs" symbolically John speaks of 1260 days which are identical to 3 ½ times and 42 months. When Daniel was using these symbols he was speaking of a period or condition of persecution. Daniel also spoke of a period of remaining faithful for 1290 days (Dan 12:11). Each of these time "periods" of 1260 days, *et al*, are symbols of a *period* or better still *conditions* of persecution. The point in passages such as Daniel 7 and 12 and Rev 11 is not *when* this condition will take place but *what does it mean*.

It is important to remember that the apocalyptic genre is not primarily interested in *time sequences* or *when* questions, but focuses rather on *what* questions and *denotation* answers (*denotation, something, such as a sign or symbol that denotes; something signified or referred to; the particular meaning of a symbol.*) In apocalyptic contexts one should ask temporal symbols *what does this mean or denote* rather than *when does it take place?*

When speaking of 1260 days as a symbol of persecution I prefer to speak of a *condition* of persecution rather than a *period* since *period* tends to be related to time rather than *condition*.

Drawing on the analogy of Ezekiel, Zechariah, and Daniel, John explains that the saints will face *a condition of persecuted* but God would protect them and ultimately vindicate them. Their *outer court* (their physical life) will be destroyed, but *the inner temple* (the saints inner spiritual, faithful, worshipping life) would be protected.

God's "two witnesses" (the martyrs, symbolized by two faithful witnesses representing truth and faithfulness) will witness faithfully throughout these "1260 days" or condition of persecution. (Notice the lesson in the next section Rev 11:4-14. For their faithfulness the martyred saints are raised and vindicated by God. Notice the connection of Rev 11:11, 12 to Ezek 37:1-14; the connection is to Ezekiel's dry bones, the head bone connected to the neck bone, etc. John is obviously drawing on the imagery and meaning of Ezek 37:1-14. In the end of Ezekiel's fascinating story a breath from God comes upon the valley of death and the saints came alive to be a great host.)

## The Two Olive trees and Two Lampstands (Rev 11:4-14)

In this section John is at his creative best! He pulls together several images from the Old Testament that highlight the faithfulness of the prophets. Using these images he paints a picture of faithful witnesses whom God protects. The intention is that the martyrs like the two olive trees and two lampstands of old, bear faithful witness for God, die, and are brought to life by the power of God to form a mighty army. We will encounter this army later at Rev 14:1-5, standing on mount Zion with the Lamb.

We should remember from our Old Testament studies that at the voice of two witnesses, truth is established. Cf. Deut 19:15. In a skillful manner John picks up the image of two trees and lampstands from Zechariah 3 and 4 and other significant texts relating to faithful prophets. The King Zerubbabel and Priest Joshua who Zechariah references were faithful witnesses for God. John also draws on Elijah and the prophets of Baal on Mount Carmel from 1 Kings 18; Ezekiel's prophecy of dry bones, Ezek 37; Abraham and Sodom and Gomorrah, Gen 18; Moses and the Egyptian plagues, Ex 7ff; the crucifixion of Jesus and the destruction of Jerusalem, Matt 24ff; and several other OT references. Skillfully John paints a fascinating picture of Rome as an evil nation that is doomed for destruction. Rome attacks the saints and conquers them only in turn to be themselves conquered for killing God's witnesses. The point is, Rome incorporates all of the evil of Sodom, Egypt, and Jerusalem and will be judged accordingly, but throughout all this God still has faithful witnesses whom he ultimately will protect even if they in passing they have to die as martyrs.

Throughout this fascinating collage of passages and images John draws on stress that God has never failed his faithful prophets in the past, and will not now fail them. Furthermore, God has in the past never failed to judge the nations that persecute his people.

Now we are ready for the climactic sounding of the seventh warning trumpet of judgment! In the previous block of material John has argued that God is loyal to his faithful witnesses and will bring them back to life again in the end time resurrection. In fact, they are assured of their resurrection even before the end time resurrection. John will argue in Revelation that the martyred saints in fact are already reigning with the victorious Christ! From out space-time continuum and perspective the eschatological resurrection lies still in the future. However, the martyrs have left our space-time continuum and are already with God in heaven! They are already reigning with Christ!

This fascinating paragraph assures the saints that God will not fail his faithful witnesses!

# The Seventh Warning Trumpet of Judgment (Rev 11:15-19)

The reader should go back to Rev 9:20 to pick up the train of thought. God was about to judge those who refused to repent of their blasphemy and murder and persecution of the saints. The seventh and last trumpet of judgment remained to be sounded! High expectation had called for an Interlude. John had provided this Interlude in Rev 10:1-11 and 11:1-14. The seventh trumpet needed to be sounded to bring the trumpets to a conclusion.

One background to the seven trumpet imagery is Joshua 6 and the fall of Jericho. Seven trumpets even in Joshua implied divine intervention! However, to our surprise there is no sound of judgment in this trumpet, only the sound of the rejoicing of the 24 elders in heaven who sat on their thrones before God. (Rev 4, the martyred saints of all time)! In honor and worship the elders fall on their faces and worship God.

## The Text

Rev 11:16-19

"And the twenty-four elders who sit on their thrones before God fell on their faces and worshiped God, $^{17}$ saying, "We give thanks to thee, Lord God Almighty, who art and who wast, that thou hast taken thy great power and begun to reign. $^{18}$ The nations raged, but thy wrath came, and the time for the dead to be judged, for rewarding thy servants, the prophets and saints, and those who fear thy name, both small and great, and for destroying the destroyers of the earth."

$^{19}$ Then God's temple in heaven was opened, and the ark of his covenant was seen within his temple; and there were flashes of lightning, voices, peals of thunder, an earthquake, and heavy hail."

The point is that God has taken his great power and exercised his sovereign reign over the nations and judged the enemies of the saints! His decisive judgment of the nations, indeed Rome, and his vindication of the saints was cause for great celebration.

Here comes the tricky part! Are we reading here at Rev 11:15ff of the final eschatological judgment? We should remember that Revelation is not about the end of the world, but about the crises about to descend on the saints. It speaks of their suffering and persecution at the hands of those who dwell on earth (those who persecute the saints, who worship the beast, and who receive the mark of the beast, Rev 13:12-18). It speaks also of the vindication of the saints. It speaks of the proleptic expectation of the judgment of Rome and the false prophet in advance of the end of the world. God's judgment of Rome is being announced in advance of the end according to God's plan!

This fascinating scene or trumpet vision demonstrates that God will bring his judgment on the saints' enemies, and that they have already been judged with end of the world judgment. Remember, in the apocalyptic genre and Revelation, present situations are viewed by God with end of the world implications and significance. To demonstrate the severity of God's judgment on those who dwell on earth, and the extent of his reward and vindication of the faithful saints, flashes of lightning, and an earthquake and heavy hail come right from the ark of God's covenant, indicating God's sovereignty, power, and faithfulness to his covenants with his people.

## Lessons We Learn from This Chapter, the Second Interlude, and 7th Trumpet

- The narrative begins with John being told to eat a small scroll which will taste both bitter and sweet! This draws on Ezekiel's eating a small scroll at Ezek 32:8-3:3. John is told that he must again prophesy too many people. There is more to be told in this story!
- A major point is that God promises to protect his faithful witnesses. They may die for their faithful testimony, but God preserves them into eternity.
- Remember the promises to the conquerors of the seven churches of Rev 2 and 3. They would eat food for

eternal life, receive crowns, and sit on thrones with Jesus.
- The story of John's scroll is that the message of Revelation has both a bitter and a sweet side, bitter in that the saints will suffer for their faith in Jesus, and sweet in that God will rescue them and raise them to sit with Jesus on thrones, judging the nations.
- God has never failed his prophets in the past and he has never failed to judge those who persecute his people. He will not fail to vindicate his saints in Asia, and even so today.
- Rev 11 builds on this theme of God's faithfulness to his saints, the church.
- When the seventh and final trumpet is sounded rather than seeing doom and destruction which was obviously to be part of God's judgment on the enemies of the church, we see rejoicing over the fact that God has taken his great power and exercised his reign over the earth.
- But the story or the message must go on!
- We pick up the second half of the story in Rev 12-22.

## Our Next Chapter

Rev 12 begins the story or preaching that God had spoken of at Rev 1:11, "You must again prophesy about many peoples and nations and tongues and kings."

In this, the second act of the drama of Revelation, John will retell or give a rebirth of images to the narrative he has been unfolding. It is the same story of crises, oppression, faithfulness, martyrdom, and victory, but is told in greater specificity. John will explain that although the enemy of the saints was still Satan, Rome had become the agent of Satan in his battle with God and the church.

# Chapter 9

# The Christ and Victory – The Climax of Revelation: Rev 12

## Introduction

This chapter brings us to the high point or climax of the message of Revelation. Refer back to chapter 2 of this commentary and the chiastic diagram depicting the structure of Revelation. It focuses on Jesus and demonstrates that through faith in Jesus and a willingness to die for one's faith one can and does conquer Satan. Martyrdom associated with faith in Jesus and his death on the cross assures the saints of victory.

The point is that Jesus is the answer to the problem of evil and suffering since in Jesus Christians are able to conquer evil and Satan, the source of evil.

It is important at this point that we remember the little scroll that John was told to eat, Rev 10:8-11!

The background John draws on for describing this message was obviously Ezek 2:8-3:3 where Ezekiel was told to eat a scroll and then prophesy. John was given a little scroll and told to eat the little scroll which would be bitter and sweet. At Rev 10:11 John is told *to prophesy again* about many peoples, nations, tongues, and kings. In other words he is told to tell the story of Revelation again.

Rev 12 begins the second act of John's drama in which he begins to *prophesy again* and retell the Revelation story, refocusing more specifically on the battle between Rome, the agent of Satan, and the church as the agent of Christ.

The story of Rev 12:1-6! Is fascinating in its symbolism! We are introduced to a woman who is expecting a male child! Rev 12:7-12 sets the scene for the chapter as well as the second act of John's drama!

At Rev 13 John will begin to focus in on Rome as the enemy and agent of Satan. We will be introduced to a terrible blasphemous beast, the political power of Rome, who rises out of the sea (a source of evil in Hebrew mythology). The beast makes war on the saints, the church, and conquers them. The reader already knows, however, that by conquering the saints they will rise again and the conqueror will in turn be conquered! (Cf. Rev 11.) We will also meet a second beast who is associated with the earth. He is the religious agent of Satan, the Roman Imperial Cult, who serves the first beast.

In telling the story of Rev 12 I will begin with Rev 12:7-12 then incorporate Rev 12:1-6 into the discussion of Rev 12:13-17.

## The War in Heaven (Rev 12:7-12)

In keeping with the Combat Mythology suggested by Adela Yarbro Collins John describes a war that arose in heaven between Michael the archangel and his angels and the dragon, Satan and his angels. In the Jewish tradition Michael is the archangel (prince of angels) who leads God's heavenly host. Michael does not lose battles! No one can defeat Michael and the heavenly host! Not even Satan! Satan and his angels are defeated and cast out of heaven – down to earth. The symbolism is that Satan is defeated in heaven and transfers his anger to God's people on earth.

The reader will be tempted to ask *when* this war took place! Again we point out that the apocalyptic genre, of which Revelation is a representative literature, does *not ask when* questions, but *asks what* questions! The point is not when this war happened, but *what does it mean*.

In the context of Revelation it means that Satan has already been defeated in heaven, he has already been defeated on earth by the death and resurrection of Jesus, and will also be defeated on earth in his efforts to destroy the church. The triumphant victory song of heaven that follows Satan being defeated by Michael, Rev 12:10ff is significant and central to the message of Revelation. Victory over Satan comes through the blood of

Christ (the cross) and the faithful testimony (martyrdom) of the saints.

This song of victory (Rev 12:10ff) is so important that I am citing it in full here to draw attention to a couple of noteworthy points.

> "And I heard a loud voice in heaven, saying, "Now the *salvation* and the power and the kingdom of our God and the authority of his Christ have come, for the accuser of our brethren has been thrown down, who accuses them day and night before our God. [11] And *they have conquered him* by the blood of the Lamb and *by the word of their testimony*, for *they loved not their lives even unto death*. [12] Rejoice then, O heaven and you that dwell therein! But woe to you, O earth and sea, for the devil has come down to you in great wrath, because he knows that his time is short!"

I have italicized certain words for emphasis and for comment that follows. I have previously observed that the Greek word *sotēria* can be translated with several different nuances according to context. In the "combat" context in which we find it here in Revelation and especially Rev 12 it should be understood as *victory*.

At the beginning of the next scene, after having been defeated in heaven, the devil is cast down to earth and begins his war on the church. In this scene John explains the recent crises of the church, notably in Asia, as the frustration of Satan as he seeks to destroy God's work on earth. A major point is that as Satan has been defeated in heaven, he will be defeated on earth.

As mentioned previously the theology of Rev 12 ties in well with Rom 8:37ff where Paul in typical apocalyptic tradition concludes his discussion of the whole creation waiting expectantly for the "arrival of the sons of God" with the statement that Christians are more than *conquerors* in Christ.

Perhaps the leading thought in this text is that martyrdom when suffered for the right reason, that is, faithfulness to God and dying for Christ, draws on the power of Jesus' death and resurrection and assures Christians of a similar resurrection and consequent victory over the powers responsible for their suffering and death. In similar fashion baptism, as a *proleptic experience* of death and resurrection unites the Christian with Christ in a death and resurrection like his. This prefigures what John is stating theologically at Rev 12 (cf. Rom 6:1-11). It is also interesting that Paul in Rom 8 at the conclusion of his apocalyptic/eschatological discourse remarks "If the Spirit of him who raised Jesus from the dead dwells in you, he who raised Christ Jesus from the dead will give life to your mortal bodies also through his Spirit which dwells in you."

## The Dragon is Cast Down to Earth and Pursues the Woman who had Given Birth to the Male Child (Rev 12:1-6; 13-17)

Displaying his artistic style John began the chapter by introducing a woman who gives birth to a male child. At first glance one might think this is a symbol of Mary, the mother of Jesus. Closer examination of the text reveals that this woman is a symbol of the Jewish messianic community who were living in faithful expectation of the coming of the Messiah. The woman who gave birth to the male child is therefore clearly a symbol of the faithful Jewish messianic community. But the story moves on and this woman has now become a different messianic community! She is the messianic community after the birth of the Messiah, the persecuted yet faithful church!

It does not take much imagination to see that the male child is the Messiah, Jesus. In keeping with the gospel story of Jesus, he is taken up to be with God. The concept of Jewish mysticism and the Enoch chariot experience resonates through this text. Those faithful to God are caught up to be with God! John adds the interesting statement that the exalted Son now rules with a rod of iron, drawing on Ps 2, the psalm of kingly ascent. John is obviously also drawing attention back to Rev 2:26ff where Jesus had promised the conquerors that they would receive a rod of iron to reign over the nations.

The Woman, now a symbol of the church, flees from the dragon into the wilderness on the *two wings of the great eagle where she will be protected by God.* The symbolism is striking! Cf. the Exodus typology of Ex 19:4 where God spoke to Israel

"You have seen what I did to the Egyptians, and how I bore you on eagles' wings and brought you to myself." The obvious implication is that God can take care of his church just as he did Israel when Israel fled from Pharaoh and Egypt. The "Woman" will be nourished and protected for 1260 days. Remember, 3 ½ years, or 42 months, and 1260 days are symbols a period of persecution, cf. Dan 7 & 12).

The dragon was angry with the "Woman" and her offspring, the church, and begins to make war on them.

In Rev 13 we will see that the dragon, Satan, does this through the civil and religious power of Rome. Notice the parallels to Dan 7. At the close of this scene at the end of Rev 12 we see the dragon standing on the sand of the sea from where he calls out a monstrous sea beast. The Jewish tradition saw the sea beast as the epitome of evil, and identified this beast as Leviathan. Leviathan in the Jewish tradition thus became a representative or form of evil and Satanic power (cf. Ps 74:13,14; 104:26; Job 3:8; 41:1; Isa 27:1; 2 *Esdras* 6:49, 52, and other Jewish sources).

## What we learn from This Chapter

- Remember, Revelation tells the story of God's plan to redeem his creation from the hold of Satan, and how God will judge and destroy evil. The story is told in a religious drama full of symbolic idiom drawn from the OT and other Jewish and early Christian traditional literature such as the Apocrypha and Pseudepigrapha.
- Revelation 12-22 repeats the story we have been following in different ways. Remember, in Rev 10 John was given a little scroll to eat. Its message was bitter and sweet. The saints would have to suffer because of their faith in Jesus, but in the end they would be rewarded by God and turn out to be the conquerors. At Rev 10:11 John was told to again tell his story.
- Rev 12-21 is the retelling of the story in greater specificity, focusing on Rome and the Church. This is the same story John had been telling through Rev 2-11.

- John now focuses attention on Satan, the dragon, who we will see in the next chapter will use the power of the Roman Empire and pagan Imperial Cult of Rome and Asia in his battle against the church. Oppression and persecution of a variety of types are the agents or means that Satan uses to get the saints to compromise their faith in God and Jesus.
- Rev 12 begins with the story of the suffering Messianic community giving birth to the Messiah, and then escaping into the wilderness where she will be protected by the power of God. God wants his church to know that in spite of Satan's efforts he will keep them safe. They may have to die for their faith but even in death God promises victory.
- The emphasis in the following chapters will be on Satan at war with God's people, determined to destroy God's plan and Savior, the Messiah.
- Symbolically, Satan and his angels have from very early been involved in a battle with God and his angels. We have no details of this age long battle, but the message about Michael informs us that Satan will be defeated in the future just as he has in the past!
- The saints need assuring that the battle is a futile battle since Satan simply cannot win! The vision of Satan's battle with Michael the archangel at Rev 12:7 sets the scene.
- The story proceeds with Satan moving his action down to earth where he does his best to thwart God's plan of redemption through the faithful remnant of Israel, the Messiah, and then the church, making war on the church. However, we know that in the end he cannot win!
- Satan takes his wrath out on God's people. In Revelation, notably Rev 13, we will see Satan using Rome and the persecution of the churches of Asia, but repeatedly God assures the saints that he will protect them. They may have to die for their faith, but in the

- end they will be the conquerors. This is the story of Revelation!
- However, during the period of persecution depicted by Satan pursuing the woman into the wilderness (symbolically represented as 3 ½ times, 42 months, and 1260 days from Dan 17 and 12) God will protect his people if they stay faithful to him and Jesus. This is the story of the Woman flying into the wilderness on the wings of an eagle (Ex 19:4).
- The scene shifts at Rev 12:17 and Rev 13:1 to Satan standing on the sand of the sea "calling" a monstrous beast up from the sea. Remember, in Canaanite and early Jewish tradition, the sea was a source of evil, and Leviathan (the evil beast) swam around in the sea (Ps 74:14; *et al*).
- In Christ evil and Satan are conquered.

## Our Next Chapter

In chapter 13 we will be introduced to two beasts who serve Satan. The sea beast makes war on the saints and the land beast supports him in this. The sea beast represent the civil power of Rome; the land beast the Imperial Cult of Rome.

# Chapter 10

# The Two Beasts and the Lamb: Revelation 13 & 14

## Introduction

John draws attention now in his drama to two beasts and a lamb. Setting the three images in parallel is interesting in that it explains to the saints that they do have a choice, either the two beast of Satan or the Lamb of God. The contrast of the two beasts and the Lamb is intentional.

In Rev 12 we saw Satan, the Dragon attempting to defeat God's purpose in the Messiah. He tried to destroy God's Messianic communities of faith; the one awaiting the birth of the Messiah, the other the church as the woman fleeing into the wilderness to be protected during persecution by the power of God. Images from the Old Testament Exodus give meaning to the story.

In the symbolic cosmic drama John was presenting we saw Satan going to war with Michael and being defeated. We saw Satan then coming down to earth in his battle against the church. We rejoiced in the voice of victory "Now the salvation and the power and the kingdom of our God and the authority of his Christ have come, for the accuser of our brethren has been thrown down, who accuses them day and night before our God. And they have conquered him by the blood of the Lamb and by the word of their testimony, for they loved not their lives even unto death."

Rev 12 closes and Rev 13 opens with Satan standing on the sands of the sea and calling a beast out of the sea. The sea in Canaanite and Jewish mythology represented one of the sources of evil. We will learn that the other mythological source of evil is the bottomless pit or the abyss. The beast that comes up out of the sea must, therefore, be evil.

## The Beast from the Sea (Rev 13:1-10)

The beast rising from the sea is described in symbols drawn from Dan 7 (notably Dan 7:19-27), where Daniel's beast made war on the saints but was defeated by the one like a son of man. Dan 7 plays a major role in John's drama in drawing an analogy to Daniel's beast that makes war on the saints but is defeated by one like the son of man who receives an everlasting kingdom.

Jewish mythology described an evil sea beast as Leviathan (cf. Job 41:1, Ps 74:13,14; 104:26; Job 3:8; 41:1; Isa 27:1; 2 Esdras 6:49, 52, and other Jewish sources). John's beast like Daniel's has seven heads and horns and 10 diadems. By analogy, John's beast must, therefore, be an oppressive national or political power since the beasts of Daniel represent oppressive national powers.

From our studies in church history the oppressive nation and political power the church faced in the 1st century AD was Rome. This beast of Rev 13:1-10, therefore, represents the political power of the Roman Empire and Emperor.

One head of the beast seemed to have a mortal wound that was healed. This represented the widespread Nero Redivivus myth feared by many concerned Romans, Jews, and Christians regarding Nero returning to continue his evil works.

This beast of Rev 13 utters blasphemous things against God. We learn that Emperor Domitian claimed to be a divine being, asserting that he was *dominus dixit*, "I am God", or *dominus et dues*, "Lord and God", and *dominus et dues noster*, "our Lord and God"!

This beast from the sea, Leviathan, makes war on the saints and conquerors them. All who *dwell on the earth* are those who worship the beast. These *who dwell on the earth* do not have their names written in the Lambs book of life. As Revelation develops we learn that *those who dwell on earth* do not represent *everyone* on earth but *those who worship the beast, who persecute the saints*, and *who will be judged for their sinister deeds*.

The fascinating poem at Rev 13:10 which is stylistically drawn from Isa 33:1 and Jer 15:2, 43:11 declares that some things such as oppression and persecution are inevitable.

*If anyone is to be taken captive,*
*to captivity he goes;*
*if anyone slays with the sword,*
*with the sword must he be slain.*

One lesson we learn from this today is that we live in a world marred by sin and a world which as a result suffers under the consequences of sin. We live in a sin filled earth in which death, suffering, illness, and other threats are inevitable as long as Satan is still operating. Revelation also teaches us, however, that Satan has already been judged in advance of the final judgment by God. Finally, in God's time he will be banished to hell or the lake of fire which is the second death. Until then Christians must remain resolute in their opposition to Satan and in their faith in God.

The application of this poem to the message of Revelation is that in the context of Rome and an evil world persecution and martyrdom were inevitable for saints who refuse to compromise their faith in Jesus.

*John adds that this poem is a call to faithfulness on the part of the saints.*

## The Beast from the Earth (Rev 13:11-18)

John next saw a second beast rising from the earth. Jewish mythology, drawing from Job 40:15 described this beast as Behemoth. Like Leviathan he was demonic. In a fascinating Russian satirical novel ca. 1920, *The Master and Margarita*, Mikhail Bulgakov depicts Satan appearing with several henchmen, one of whom is Behemoth. Behemoth and the other henchman carry out Satan's dirty work! Bulgakov understood the symbolism of these two beasts and especially Behemoth.

The earth or land beast looks like a lamb but speaks like a dragon. It represents the religious power of the Imperial Cult, but is satanic in power. Behemoth draws its power and authority from the first beast, Leviathan, the Roman Imperial power.

The earth beast causes men to worship the first beast and deceives people by great signs. Those who are deceived and worship the beast are those *"who dwell on the earth"*, a synonym in Revelation for those who follow the Imperial Cult, worship the first beast, and persecute the saints.

Those who worship the first beast receive the mark of the beast on their right hand and forehead. Remember Rev 7:3, those who belong to God and are protected by God receive his mark on their foreheads. We will see that those who are with the Lamb in Rev 14:1ff have received his mark and the mark of God on their foreheads (cf. Ex 12:23 and Ezek 9:1ff, especially 9:4).

The mark of the beast is symbolically 666! We must understand the symbolism of Gematria in ancient times, and the symbolic use of numbers in Revelation. Gematria is a "game" one plays by giving a numerical number to letters of the alphabet in a form of secret code. This phenomenon was common in the ancient world, especially among the Greeks, Jews, and Romans.

Much speculation has been given to attempts to identify this number with Nero, Claudius, the Pope, Hitler, and any other sinister person who has become the enemy of the saints or church. All in vain! The numbers just don't work! To get the number to point to Nero one has to work off the Hebrew alphabet. The problem with this is that Revelation was written in Greek, not Hebrew, and the Hebrew alphabet does not have vowels leading to issues with the Latin name Nero which includes two vowels!

The *Sibylline Oracles* (Jewish and Christian apocalyptic writings ca. BC 150 to 150AD) 1:324ff, and early Christian Gematria, identify Jesus' name with the number 888! (Greek Ἰησοῦς *Iesous*, Ἰ=10, η=8, σ= 200, o=70, ῦ=400, ς=200 Ἰησοῦς = 888.)

Whatever John's purpose, the beast's number does not include 7 and is less than Jesus' number 888! However, John does not leave us in a mystery, he tell us that 666 is a *man's or human number*! *The beast then is a human being, not a divine being.* To worship a human being with the number of 666 as a god is both foolish and blasphemous!

The point of this little game of 666 is that it is associated with the religious power of the Imperial Cult and those who worship the Sea Beast or Roman Civil power or the emperor receive this number. It is a human number not a divine number telling us that the emperor is a human being not a divine being! So why worship a human being?

## The Lamb on Mount Zion at Rev 14:1-5

In contrast to the two evil beasts of Rev 13 John then saw the Lamb standing on Mount Zion. Mount

Zion was a part of the city of Jerusalem, the traditional place from where God's kings of Israel after David ruled, and where the temple was located. The implication is that it is Jesus, the Lamb of God, who is ruling over God's creation and kingdom, not the Emperor of Rome. The saints must choose whether they would be members of the Roman "kingdom" or empire, or members of God's kingdom over which Jesus reigned.

At Rev 5:5 the Lamb was pictured as the Lion of the Tribe of Judah, and the Root of David, both are royal Messianic terms. John introduced the reader early on to the fact that it was Jesus who ruled over God's kingdom, and it was only Jesus who could unravel and reveal the mystery of God's plan.

The Lamb was standing on Mount Zion with the 144,000, that is, those who were faithful to him and who comprised his church militant and victorious (Cf. Rev 7:1-17). They are described in military terms (Rev 14:4ff). The background to this numbering was Israel's understanding that only God was permitted to number his military campaigners (sign of faith in God). The numbering was also a sign of God knowing who belonged to him. The concept of being chaste (Rev 14:4) drew on the understanding that before Israel's army went out on a campaign as God's army they took an oath of chastity (cf. 1 Sam 21:4, 5; Deut 20; Deut 23:9, 10).

The 144,000 have been sealed (ownership and protection) with the seal of God in contrast to those who worship the beast (the Roman Emperor) and have received his human number and mark (666) on their foreheads.

We will encounter this militant group and the Lamb again in the triumphant scene of the Rider on the White Horse (Rev 19:11-16) judging the defeated beast and false prophet.

The point here, in the context of Revelation as Combat Mythology, the 144,000 represent God's army, the church both militant and victorious (Rev 7:3-8 and Rev 14:1-5). They are in a war with Satan and Rome. They will die as martyrs, but they are conquerors and stand with Jesus on Mount Zion where they share in his reign.

## The Interlude of Rev 14:6-20

This interlude, like the other interludes, is introduced to interrupt the flow of thought and make a significant point. This interlude introduces seven angels with important messages for Rome, for those who worship the Emperor, and for the saints. John numbers the first three angelic messages and then leaves the numbering of the remaining four to the reader. Stipulating seven angelic messages when only three are numbered is interesting but not vital! There are obviously more than three angelic messages in this text. We pick the number seven because this is Revelation and things get done in sevens in Revelation!

*Message One:* God appeals to those who worship the Emperor one more time; repent, fear God and give him the glory, do not worship Rome or the emperor. These are those who John refers to as those *who dwell on the earth*.

*Message Two:* The message is that Babylon/Rome, like Babylon of old, has fallen. This indicates that God has already judged Rome with the same judgment he brought on Babylon of old. Rome has seduced the nations and made them drunk with her power and for this she will be judged.

*Message Three:* Those who worship the beast and receive his mark will drink the wine of God's wrath and be judged with eternal punishment. This is a warning call to the saints for faithful endurance.

*Message Four:* Blessed are those who die in the Lord. He has reference here to the faithful saints who die as martyrs. The principle is generally true.

*Message Five:* An angel calls for the judgment of those who worship the beast. The sickle is a symbol of divine judgment.

*Message Six:* Another angel appears also with the sickle repeating the message of divine judgment.

*Message Seven:* An angel begins the judgment of Babylon/Rome. Symbolizing the extent of God's judgment on Rome, blood flows as high as a horses bridle for over 200 miles!

## What we learn from this Chapter and Rev 13 and 14

- John identifies the sinister nature of the Roman Empire; it is a terrifying beast similar to the beast of Dan 7. This beast rises out of the sea, the sea being a symbol of an evil source.
- We learn that this beast represents the civil and political power of Rome, is the agent of Satan.
- This beast will persecute (make war on the saints) and has a blasphemous character. The beast is blasphemous in that he sets himself up as a god.
- This beast has an additional character! He is accompanied by a second beast, a religious beast, (the Imperial Cult) that causes people to worship the first beast. Those who worship the beast are identified as those *who dwell on the earth.*
- Christians must choose which number or seal they wish to be identified by, the number of the beast, 666, which is a human number, or the seal or number of the Lamb!
- Notice the contrast between the two evil beasts and the Lamb. The sea beast sits in Rome while the Lamb is on Mount Zion as the true ruler of God's kingdom.
- Seven angelic messages call for repentance, the worship of God, and pronounce judgment on those who worship the beast. This is a warning and call to the saints for faithful endurance.

- The main point is that the saints must choose who they will worship; the beast of the sea, Rome, the agent of Satan, or Jesus God's sovereign ruler of all creation.

## Our Next Chapter

Previously God had sent warning judgments on Rome intending these judgments to bring Rome to repentance. But Rome had refused.

In the next chapter we will see God's warning judgments consummated on Rome. Rome is now pronounced as judged by God with final judgment.

# Chapter 11
# God's Judgment on Rome Consummated: Revelation 15-19

## Introduction

In an earlier section (Chapter 7, Rev 8, 9) God had sent warning judgments (trumpets) on Rome calling on Rome to repent of her evil deeds and the persecution of the saints. In this section we will see God's judgments described as consummated as the Beast and False Prophet are judged by God. In order to drive home the severity of God's judgment on Rome John describes this in end of the world language. This is another of John's literary and theological techniques, and an example of proleptic eschatological judgments in which a present situation of judgment is described in end of the world language to emphasize the severity and completeness of God's present judgment. Historically, the final judgment is still future, but theologically God has already judged Rome with end of the world judgment and severity.

Since the concept of a proleptic eschatological judgment is difficult for some to grasp, and since we are prone to looking for temporal issues in our study of Revelation I stress that this section does not describe the final end of the world. It only describes God's judgments on Rome in final end of the world language for dramatic emphasis. God is taking Rome's sin and evil seriously. He is demonstrating in graphic terms his vindication of the saints suffering and martyrdom. The point is that God has already judged Rome with final judgment!

Note particularly that this judgment is on the Beast (Rome in its civil power) and the False Prophet (the Imperial Cult which seduced people to worship the Beast, Rome). Both are metaphors describing some aspect of Rome's actions.

## The Heavenly Vision and the Seven Bowls of God's Wrath (Rev 15:1-16:21)

The heavenly vision of Rev 15 is similar in style and theology to the heavenly vision of Rev 4. It is important for the reader to understand that the judgment on Rome about to be pronounced comes right from the throne room of God. In this scene we see those who have conquered the beast and the false prophet singing a hymn of praise to God, for his judgments are just and righteous. They are standing beside the sea (the sea being a Canaanite and Hebrew symbol of evil) as in Rev 4. The sea is glasslike! It holds no threats for the saints that have conquered! They were singing the song of Moses and the Lamb, a song of deliverance from the new "Egypt", Rome. Rome no longer holds any threat for these saints who have conquered. I have italicized certain expressions for emphasis. Notice that the first three emphasize the righteousness, sovereignty, and holiness of God. The last one stresses that his judgments are now revealed.

"Great and wonderful are thy deeds,
O Lord God the Almighty!
*Just and true are thy ways,*
*O King of the ages*! [4] Who shall not fear and glorify thy name, O Lord?
*For thou alone art holy.*
All nations shall come and worship thee,
*for thy judgments have been revealed.*"

Seven angels with seven bowls of God's wrath appear (Rev 15:5). They have been given by one of the four living creatures seven bowls which are full of the wrath of God. This emphasizes that God's judgments are right and are associated with the holiness of God.

The seven bowls contain seven plagues reminiscent of the Exodus plagues and God's judgment on Egypt. These plagues are to be poured out on those who dwell on earth, that is, those who oppose God and his purpose and oppress his people. They are also those who have worshipped the beast. A voice coming right out of the temple of God instructs the angels to pour out the contents of the bowls of the wrath of God.

*Bowl One*: (Rev 16:2). Foul and evil sores break out on those who bore the mark of the beast and who worship the beast.

*Bowl Two*: (Rev 16:3). The sea becomes like blood and everything living in the sea dies. Remember the plagues on the waters of Egypt.

*Bowl Three*: (Rev 16:4-7). A Third of the waters become blood. There is a cry from the altar connecting this plague with a response to the prayers of the saints which came from beneath the altar, prayers for their vindication (Rev 6:10). This righteous judgment vindicates the saints! It is important to see the connection John makes with the prayers of the saints at Rev 6:10.

*Bowl Four*: (Rev 16:8, 9). Fierce heat from the sun scorches those who oppose God, but in response they only curse God indicating their unrepentant hearts. They refuse to give God the glory. This possibly connects to their determination to worship the emperor.

*Bowl Five*: (Rev 16:10, 11). The kingdom of Rome is in darkness and fear indicating internal turmoil. This fear and turmoil must be seen comparison to the glorious kingdom of God. Rome is weak and insecure, God's kingdom powerful and secure.

*Bowl Six*: (Rev 16:12-16). This is the second reference to Babylon as a euphemism for Rome. John will build on this symbolism in the following chapters illustrating that as God had taken care of Babylon so he will take care of Rome; as Babylon fell to the Medes (Jer 50:35-40; 51:11) so Rome, the new Babylon, will fall. The nations following Rome assemble at *Har Megiddo* (the Greek for Armageddon) which symbolizes a traditional place of battle in Israel. This slight mount and ancient Israeli fortress was near the plain of Jezreel where great battles were fought and won by Israel. Armageddon, like Waterloo, symbolizes defeat of the enemy and victory for God's people. As surely as Napoleon was defeated at Waterloo, so surely Rome and Satan will be defeated at *Har Megiddo*, Armageddon! Most nations have places of symbolic battles won or lost that become symbols for wider reference. For Americans Pearl Harbor, Normandy, or the Alamo would be such places that took on greater meaning than the original battle. *Har Megiddo* was such a symbolic referent.

*Bowl Seven*: (Rev 16:17-21). With great apocalyptic signs symbolic of God's judgment of ancient nations, God pronounces his judgment on Babylon/Rome. A loud voice from the temple of God announced "It is done!" God has judged Rome in advance of the final end with end of the world significance. The saints have been vindicated!

## The Great Harlot and the Mystery of the Seven Kings of Rome who are in fact Eight Kings! (Rev 17:1-18)

Rev 17 is one more vision John gives the reader, focusing in on the extent of God's judgment on Rome, and explaining the reason for such judgments. This vision emphasizes the extent of Rome's sin.

John refers to Rome as Babylon the mother of harlots Rev 17:4-6:

> "The woman was arrayed in purple and scarlet, and bedecked with gold and jewels and pearls, holding in her hand a golden cup full of abominations and the impurities of her fornication; [5] and on her forehead was written a name of mystery: "Babylon the great, mother of harlots and of earth's abominations." [6] And I saw the woman, drunk with the blood of the saints and the blood of the martyrs of Jesus."

This is a highly symbolic text. It is important to grasp the symbolism John uses as he describes the awful power and sin of Rome. Repeatedly throughout Revelation John uses several symbols or euphemisms to describe the character of Rome. He speaks of Rome as a sea beast, Leviathan, a land beast, Behemoth, the beast and the false prophet, a great harlot, and Babylon.

The Great Harlot represents the Roman Imperial Cult (the religious power of Rome). The Great Harlot is another metaphor for the land beast, Behemoth, who seduces and convinces men to worship the Emperor of Rome, the Sea Beast (Rev 13). The land beast, or Behemoth, as a religious cult is also a great harlot who seduces people to worship the beast from the sea. Rome is intoxicated by its power and ability to seduce people and make war on and kill the saints.

John marvels at the mystery of the woman whom he has depicted as a great harlot (Rev 17:6). An angel explains this mysterious symbolism to John. The explanation itself is also highly symbolic and needs its own explanation! The mystery involves seven and eight kings. Obviously the meaning of the great harlot seated on the scarlet beast has reference to the Imperial Cult riding on the power of the Emperor or civil power of Rome

In the angel's explanation, seven kings come and go, one is like Nero. The "one who was, and is not, and who is to ascend from the bottomless pit and go on to perdition" (ruin) is a reference to the Nero Redivivus myth (a myth that held that Nero was not really dead and would soon return to continue his evil reign). The seven kings that follow imply that they all incorporate the evil of Nero. The seventh becomes an eighth, which is the one they are about to face, most likely representing Emperor Domitian. However, all eight kings are to go on to perdition/ruin. They look fierce and powerful, but they will all be brought to ruin by the power of God.

Some commentators have tried to number the kings and identify them with the Roman Emperors, but to do so one has to take great liberty in counting the Emperors and subjectively drop those who do not fit the calculation! This altogether misses the point John is making! His point is that the king the saints are facing (Domitian) incorporates all of the evil of the preceding kings, but he too will go on to perdition/ruin!

Emphasizing the point that John is speaking symbolically, he refers to the kings as kings and not emperors! The emperors were not usually referred to as kings which in the Greek are two entirely different words.

Ten client kings (not real kings but those who rule under Rome's power – the Roman provincial governors or subject kings like Herod, for example) will follow the beast and make war on the saints. But the Lamb will also conquer them. The ten kings (ten horns) will hate Rome, indicating the internal turmoil and insecurity of Rome.

John clarifies his point by concluding by stating that the woman represents the great city Rome which has dominion over the client kings (Rev 17:18).

## The Doom of Babylon/Rome Retold (Rev 18:1-24)

Continuing the story of the demise of Rome at Rev 18:1-3 John adopts a poetic style to announce the doom of Rome in terms that describe the doom of Babylon of old.

He draws heavily on Isaiah, Jeremiah, and Ezekiel for his poetic symbols. His point is that God can destroy Babylon/Rome just as easily as he destroyed Babylon of old. In fact, he can do this in one day, even one hour! (Rev 18:8, 10).

Note that in this chapter John draws heavily on the poetic genre to tell its story. The nations and merchants mourn over the loss of Rome for their trade has been destroyed.

## The Celebration in Heaven and the Marriage Feast of the Bride and the Lamb (Rev 19:1-10)

At Rev 19:1-10 John has composed a great hymn of praise which included four Hallelujah choruses. The heavenly host, the four living creatures, and the conquering saints all sing God's praises for his judgment of the great harlot (Rome and its Imperial Cult). The hymn proclaims that God's judgments are true and just.

Notice that Rev 19:1 records a great multitude in Heaven singing, "Hallelujah! Salvation and glory and power belong to our God, $^2$ for his judgments are true and just..." It is not only salvation that the great multitude celebrates, but *victory*, pronouncing that glory and power belong to God, not Rome!

The symbol of the marriage supper of the Lamb is similar to Jesus' lesson of the marriage feast, the bridegroom, and the final judgment (cf. Matt 25:1-13). In this case the martyrs become the bride of the Lamb. The concept of banquets in ancient traditions carried significant meaning, mostly of acceptance. Jewish and Christian traditions speak of a great eschatological, end time banquet in heaven when God and Jesus will sit down with their faithful servants. In fact, the Lord's Supper is an advanced experience of this great heavenly eschatological banquet. Remember that at Rev 2:17 the conquerors were given invitations (little white stones) to the eschatological (end of the world) banquet in heaven.

A blessing is pronounced on those who are invited to share in this feast, the marriage supper of the Lamb (Rev 19:9).

## The Defeat of the Beast and the False Prophet Announced (Rev 19:11-21)

John gives the reader a further dramatic vision of God's judgment on Rome; the beast, and the false prophet. It would be a mistake to simply see this as a vision of the final judgment. It nevertheless carries in it all of the seriousness and implications of the final judgment. Here we see God carrying out in this visionary experience the judgment that the souls beneath the altar of Rev 6:10 had cried out for. The judgment of their enemies and the vindication of their faith were taking place before their eyes!

In this vision Jesus is the rider on the white horse. Our minds go back to the striking vision of Jesus at Rev 1:1ff. Now we hear that he is the Word of God, the one who is faithful and true. In Johannine tradition the Word of God had been the creator of all creation. It is He who now rides onto the stage as the conquering king. He is described in war "regalia" with a sword of judgment in his mouth.

He has a name (or character, possibly implying "conqueror") which no one knows but he himself. This unknown symbolism relates to the fact that many do not know the significance of Jesus' Lordship and reign, but he does and so do the saints! Jesus, the crucified one, not the Emperor of Rome, is King of kings and Lord of lords!

Jesus captured the beast and the false prophet (Rome in its great civil and religious power) and threw them into the lake of burning fire and sulphur (a Jewish/Christian symbol of hell or eternal punishment). He destroys those who have followed the Imperial Cult and who have worshipped the beast (Rome) and offers their flesh to the birds of the sky as a terrible feast. The birds gorge on their flesh.

Note the contrast and irony of the two feasts, one the messianic banquet which the faithful saints enjoy, the other the feast of the vultures on the flesh of the unfaithful worshippers of the beast! The birds gorge on this flesh in a horrible scene! So great and terrifying is God's judgment on Rome.

The point is, "Do you want to enjoy the messianic banquet of Jesus, or be the feast of the vultures?"

## What We Learn From this Chapter and Rev 15-19

- Although God calls every person to repent and worship him (Rev 9:20) he nevertheless will judge the unfaithful and those who serve and pay homage to Satan and his wiles.
- He warns those "who dwell on the earth" that he will judge them just as he judged Egypt (the plagues) when they will not repent.
- In this section he warns the Christians that the "king" (Emperor) with whom they are dealing incorporates all the evil of the preceding "kings" (Emperors).
- All of the Emperors will all be brought to ruin (perdition) (Rev 17:7-18).
- God announces his judgment on Rome in advance of the final end to encourage the saints.
- The saints need assurance that He has already judged Rome.
- They need encouragement not to succumb to the seductive powers of Rome and the Imperial Cult.
- There is great celebration in heaven over God's judgment of the beast and the false prophet, that is, the civil power of Rome and the Imperial Cult (Rev 15:3-8).

- John poetically describes the defeat and judgment of the beast and the false prophet whom God throws into the lake of fire which is a symbol of eternal punishment (Hell) (Rev 18).
- Those who follow and worship the beast are killed and fed to the birds of the air that gorge on their flesh!
- This feast is a stark contrast to the feast of the Bride and the lamb (Rev 19:17-21).
- The message to the saints in Asia, and to all Christians, **"Decide which feast to which you would like to be invited!"**

## Our Next Chapter

The next chapter will cover The 1000 Year Binding of Satan and Reign of the Martyrs (Rev 20).

We will be reminded to pay careful attention to John's symbolic use of numbers.

This chapter in some measure picks up Jesus' promise to conquerors in that it speaks of the saints reigning with Christ.

# Chapter 12

# The 1000 Year Binding of Satan and the Reign of the Martyrs Revelation 20:1-20:15

## Introduction

For many people this chapter is what Revelation is all about! Unfortunately that view misses the real gist or purpose of Revelation. However, it is a fascinating piece of Scripture set out in a highly symbolic genre!

In painting the picture of this vision John draws his images from a rich repository of Old Testament and Jewish apocryphal, apocalyptic, and pseudepigraphical literature. In order to understand this chapter one must remember all that we have learned from John's literary palette and style. Unfortunately, many attempt to unravel this fascinating and challenging chapter without paying attention to what John has been writing. This chapter is not where one should begin in interpreting Rev 20 and the 1000 year binding of Satan and 1000 year reign of the saints.

Some scholars have suggested that this is possibly the most difficult portion of Revelation to unravel and interpret. Unfortunately the message of Rev 20 has been covered over by highly speculative millennial views (Premillennialism, Dispensationalism, Postmillennialism, and Amillennialism) which we will briefly look at in the last lesson or addendum to this study. These millennial views are unfortunately read into the text and are not found in the text!

There is a tendency to read *time* issues (1,000 years) into the text and interpret the time elements literally. This is unfortunate since the text does not intend to set a timetable for the kingdom and reign of Christ. In fact, the 1000 year reign is not that of Christ but of the saints!

We have already noticed that numbers in Revelation are to be understood symbolically of events or conditions. This should hold true for the 1,000 year as well.

The text is mysterious and highly symbolic and poses several significant questions:
- How do you bind Satan with a great chain?
- How do you throw him into a bottomless pit, the Abyss?
- Who is reigning and where are they reigning?
- Who are Gog and Magog?

In most of our better translations this text is correctly broken into four paragraphs:
- The binding of Satan for 1,000 years (Rev 20:1-3).
- The 1,000 year reign of the martyred saints (Rev 20:4-6). This paragraph is *parenthetic* and can be read around, "parked", or held in abeyance until after Rev 20:7-10. We will do this in our notes for simplification!
- Satan is loosed from the pit to deceive other nations, but is finally judged and thrown into hell with the beast, false prophet, and those who worship the beast (Rev 20:7-10).
- The great white throne signifies God on his throne judging evil (Rev 20:11-15).

## The Binding of Satan for 1,000 years (Rev 20:1-3)

The first scene is of a powerful angel coming down out of heaven. He obviously has the authority over the Abyss or *bottomless pit* since he holds the key to the *bottomless pit*. The angel seizes the dragon, that is, Satan, and binds him with a great chain, and throws him into the bottomless pit for 1,000 years.

The Abyss or *bottomless pit* (Greek *abussos*) in Jewish mythology is traditionally understood to be one of the major sources of evil.

This is the first time in Revelation, and the only place in the New Testament where we read of Satan or an evil demon being bound with a great chain or being thrown into a bottomless pit for 1,000 years! It is obviously to be understood symbolically since you do not simply bind a spiritual being or demon or Satan with a large chain even if you are an angel from heaven! So how do we understand it? We are not at a real loss since the apocalyptic tradition has something to say about this kind of thing.

The Jewish apocryphal and apocalyptic tradition (Tobit 8; Testament of Levi 18:8-12; 1 Enoch 53:3, 54:5 et al) records the binding of evil spirits, sometimes with a chain, and either sending them out into the desert or keeping them in a deep cavern. This binding represents a limitation of their power to plague and trouble people.

In our story, Satan is bound for 1,000 years which in keeping with the above tradition would mean that he is completely limited in his ability in some way. 1,000 years represents a *complete* situation (Ps 50:10; cattle on a thousand hills belong to God, meaning all the cattle belong to God. 1,000 is 10 cubed (10x10x10) which is considered to be a complete number.

Again we encounter John using time figures. In Revelation he has already spoken of 10 years, 3 ½ years, 42 months, and 1260 days. In all these references John uses the time figures to symbolically represent some condition. In our case 1,000 is a symbol of completeness, thus 1,000 years should not be taken literally as a period of time but of a condition, just as 1260 days represented a condition of persecution.

In the context of Revelation and Rome, Satan is completely limited in his ability to *deceive the nations* (Rev 20:3, Rome and her allies), meaning that God has judged Rome and will take away her power to use the nations to achieve her purpose. Thus, 1,000 years is symbolic of Satan's condition (completely bound) and does not represent a period of time. The apocalyptic genre traditionally uses time symbolically to represent a condition.

But Satan will be released after *a little while*, meaning that he will still have the ability to use other nations for his purpose (cf. Gog and Magog of Rev 20:8).

## The Loosing of Satan after his Binding
## (Rev 20:7-10)

Remember, we have "parked" the parenthetic paragraph of Rev 20:4-6 for a few minutes to get the flow of thought from Rev 20:3. Rev 20:3 saw Satan bound and thrown into the abyss with the statement that he would be "loosed for a little while". We observed that this meant that Satan had been completely limited by God in his ability to use Rome to deceive the nations.

At the risk of redundancy or repetitive information it is necessary at this point to be reminded regarding apocalyptic and Revelation's use of numbers and time referents. Although it is difficult for modern interpreters to put a time period out of mind in favor of a statement of condition, being bound for 1,000 years is a symbol for being *completely bound*. We are reminded that the apocalyptic genre does not think in terms of time but does set its message of time out as a condition. Apocalyptic and Revelation are not really concerned with *when* questions but is involved in understanding *what* is meant by the time referent.

However, Satan continues to use other nations to carry out his deception. This is seen in John's reference to the figurative symbol of Gog and Magog. Gog was the king of an ancient nation known as Magog which in the Jewish apocalyptic tradition had come to represent the resilience of evil nations. We find this concept in the *Sibylline Oracles* and other apocalyptic sources. (Cf. Ezek 38:2; 39:1.)

Satan gathers these symbolic nations for battle against the saints (God's people), but guess what? He and they are defeated! (Cf. Rev 20:11.)

Then Satan, the devil and deceiver of the nations is thrown into the lake of fire that burns with sulphur. In the Jewish tradition this represents hell! There the devil joins the beast, the civil Rome, and the false prophet, the harlot or Imperial Cult, (Rev 19:19) where they will be tormented forever and ever!

## The 1,000 Year Reign (Rev 20:4-6)

Now we return to the parenthetical paragraph of Rev 20:4-7. This is where the Premillennialists and Dispensationalists abuse Scripture! They simply do not read what John is saying and read their interpretation into the text! From this passage they conclude that Christ will return to the earth and reign on earth for 1,000 years!

This paragraph and its statements are admittedly difficult but they do make sense if we do not read into the text issues that are contrary to the text and keep the text within the symbolism of Revelation and the apocalyptic tradition!

*First*, the text clearly reads that those reigning for 1,000 years are the martyred saints, not Christ! He reigns forever in the eternal kingdom! Their reigning for 1,000 years refers to the completeness of their reigning. They have died a terrible death but now they are the conquerors and reign completely with Christ. To the degree of completeness that Satan is bound and limited, to that same degree *the saints reign completely with Christ*.

*Second*, these martyred saints are not on earth, but in heaven with God! This is what Revelation has been teaching ever since Rev 2 and 3 and the seven letters to the seven churches! They have died and gone to be with Jesus in heaven and sit with him on thrones (Cf. Rev 2:17, 27, Rev 14, 15).

The expression "*the rest of the dead did not come to life until the 1,000 year reign is ended*" has caused commentators several problems! There are several difficult questions that arise from this expression! *First*, who are the rest of the dead? Are they those who died in Christ but not by martyrdom? This might be true! Are they those who compromised their faith and worshipped the beast and received his mark? *Second*, what does it mean that they did not come to life until the 1,000 years were ended! Our tendency to think in time referents complicates our understanding of this statement. If the 1,000 years binding of Satan was a reference to the extent (completeness) of his limitation, then the rest of the dead do not share in the resurrection due to Satan's limitation and their association with him.

Although I recognize the difficulty in this text I am persuaded in favor of the last choice, those dead who did not come to life are those who worshipped the beast. They do not have their name written in the Lamb's book of life and do not share in the reign with Christ! They do not share in this first resurrection of the martyrs.

The next statement is equally difficult! *"This is the first resurrection."* What is the first resurrection?

Some argue that it is baptism (Church of Christ folk like this one, but that is Rom 6 and not Revelation!) In the context of Revelation it most likely refers to the martyrs who have been resurrected to be with Christ and God, who sit on thrones with Jesus. A blessing is pronounced over those who represent the first resurrection. John adds this to reassure the saints of their victory over Satan and Rome. They certainly suffered a terrible death but they are blessed for dying faithfully to God (cf. Rev 14:13).

Thus in my opinion, the first resurrection is best understood as representing the martyrs who have died in the Lord and have been raised to sit with Jesus on his throne (Rev 2:17, 2:27; Rev 11:4-12, notably Rev 11:12).

The *second death* (the final judgment Rev 20:12-15) has no power over them. They are safe since they have the mark of God and the Lamb on them and their names are written in the lamb's book of life. They are already reigning completely with Christ for 1,000 years.

One last comment or two! We need to keep the 1,000 year referents in parallel thought. John is intentionally demonstrating the parallel conditions of Satan, the martyrs, those who do not experience the resurrection from the dead. Satan is completely limited (bound, restrained) in his ability to use Rome permanently. The saints reign completely with Christ. Those who worship the beast have no part (completely no part) in the resurrection to be with God. Satan will continue his deception of other nations but will in the end be defeated by God and Christ and thrown into the lake of fire, that is, hell!

## The Great White Throne (Rev 20:11-15)

This is the final judgment scene! We are reminded that Revelation is not really about the final judgment. It is about a crisis about to break in on the churches in Asia. Revelation is a theodicy (the defense of the righteousness of God) but no theodicy would be complete that does not take care of and remove the source of evil (Satan) completely from human experience. John inserts this paragraph to bring closure to his story and theodicy.

The dead, great and small, are standing before God who is on his throne. *The books are opened.* In Jewish tradition this meant the books by which the world will be judged. *The book of life is opened.* Those whose names are written in the book of life have no fear of the final judgment, they belong to Jesus. They will not be judged and condemned to the lake of fire.

The sea (the source of evil in Jewish tradition and in Revelation, cf. Rev 13), death, and Hades (the place of the dead) give up their dead for judgment. Death and Hades are thrown into *the lake of fire* with Satan and those who worship the beast. This is *the second death, the final judgment.*

The sea as a source of evil is no more (Rev 21:1) because Satan is no more! There will be no more suffering, tears, death (martyrdom), and mourning, for the former system has been done away!

*All things are done.* The end has come and all things will be made new (Rev 21:5, 6). *Hallelujah!*

## What We Learn From this Chapter and Rev 20

- Wow! What a chapter!
- First, we learn that there will be a final judgment! Revelation as a theodicy must bring closure to the story.
- However, this is not the main purpose of Revelation, for Revelation is the story of the Victory of the Saints over Rome and Satan, and the reward of the saints for their faithfulness to Jesus.

- They will reign completely (for 1,000 years) with Jesus in his kingdom!
- But the story (a theodicy – the defense of the righteousness of God in the face of evil) cannot be complete while Satan still exists and can carry out his attacks on God's creation.
- Satan will be limited by God to use Rome (bound for 1,000 years), but will move on to other scenes (Gog and Magog are symbols of the resilience of evil nations).
- Satan has to be judged and the final judgment story must be told.
- In this brief paragraph John gives us a glimpse of the saints reigning in heaven with God and Christ. We are also given a glimpse of the final judgment and Satan's final condemnation to hell.
- After this judgment the sea (a source of evil) is no more!
- There is no more suffering, death, and mourning!
- Heaven is real and has come!
- All things have been completed!
- *Hallelujah!*

## Our Next Chapter

In the next chapter of our study we will examine Rev 21, 22. We will learn of the symbolic arrival of a completely new dimension of life, the new heaven and earth, the City of the Living God, and the blessings of being part of that city.

The story will end with a blessing to the saints, and a warning not to diminish or add to the message of Revelation.

We will also examine some of the theological lessons of Revelation and what we can learn from this great book.

# Chapter 13

# The Finale: Revelation 21:1-22:21

## Introduction

In this lesson we will cover the last two sections of Revelation:
1. The Church in Perfection (Rev 21:1-22:5).
2. The Epilogue (Rev 22:6-22:21).

Prologue. 1:1-20
  I. The Church in Imperfection. 2:1-3:22
        Seven Letters to the Seven Churches
      II. The Authority of God over Evil Explained. 4:1-8:6 Seven Seals on the Scroll
      III. The Warning Judgments. 8:1-11:19
      Seven Trumpets
        IV. The Lamb - God's Answer to Evil. 12:1-14:20
        Seven Unnumbered Figures
    V.   The Consummated Judgments. 15:1-16:21
      Seven Bowls of Wrath
    VI. The Authority of God over Evil Exercised. 17:1-20:15
      Seven Unnumbered Descriptions of God's Judgments
  VII. The Church in Perfection. 21:1-22:5
    Seven Unnumbered Descriptions of the Church in Perfection
Epilogue. 22:6-21

Notice that the *Prologue* matches the *Epilogue*, or is in *a parallel structure*, and that *The Church in Imperfection (section I)* is parallel to *The Church in Perfection (section VII)*.

In John's brilliant structure *The Church in Perfection* is the realization of the hopes of *The Church in Imperfection*. The

*Church in Imperfection* we read about in Rev 2 and 3, the letters to the Seven Churches in Asia. *The Church in Perfection* we might call the church having *arrived in heaven*, or *the final end of the faithful church or Christians*!

John explains that this is the promise to all faithful Christians, but his focus in Revelation is essentially and primarily on those who have conquered (the martyrs). *The idea of this section is to stress the point that those who die as martyrs have this great hope and home in heaven with God.* Because they have died in ignominy they will not be disappointed in heaven!

The *Epilogue* repeats in almost the exact words most of the major themes of the *Prologue*. We will examine these below.

*But, first*, let's discuss *The Church in Perfection!*

## The Church in Perfection (Rev 21:1-22:5): John presents this in Seven Unnumbered Descriptions of the Church in Perfection

- The New Heaven and the New Earth (Rev 21:1).
- The New Jerusalem - the Dwelling of God (Rev 21:2-8).
- The Glory of the Holy City, Jerusalem (Rev 21:9-14).
- The Measurements of the City (Rev 21:15-18).
- The Foundations of the City (Rev 21:19-21).
- The Light of the City (Rev 21:22-27).
- The Sustenance of the City (Rev 22:1-5).

## The New Heaven and New Earth (Rev 21:1)

In order to understand the reference to a new heaven and new earth one must understand the role this played in Isa 65:17 and 66:22. In the Jewish tradition a new heaven and new earth is an idiom that represents a new order of things, a new system. We find this also at 2 Pet 3:13 which is similar to Rev 21:1 in that *this new heaven and new earth is where righteousness dwells.* In Isa 65 and 66 it had reference to the Messianic age.

In Rev 21 this idiom has reference to Heaven, a new system in which there is no evil, no suffering, no death, no tears, and no weeping. In the context of the severe persecution in Asia this would have a lot of meaning!

Rev 21:1 is important in the expression that the *sea is no more*. Those understand that the sea was a source of evil would appreciate this expression. Remember in Revelation the sea is a place of evil out of which the beast [Rome] arose, Rev 13:1. To the Christians in Asia to whom Revelation was written no more sea would mean no more beast, no more persecution, and no more martyrdom!

## The New Jerusalem (Rev 21:2-8)

The old Jerusalem was a symbol of God's dwelling place and where his people lived. It was from here that David and the kings of God's kingdom reigned. By the time of writing Revelation in AD 95 the old Jerusalem and temple were no more. Jerusalem had been destroyed and the Christians scattered far and wide, even to Asia.

The New Jerusalem is the new dwelling place of the saints with God. At Rev 3:12, the New Jerusalem was the reward of faithful martyrs who had died. They had been promised a new home with God. Now in John's cosmic drama the New Jerusalem arrives out of heaven as the new city of God.

In this city God *personally* will dwell with the saints in the *fullest measure* (not as in the Tabernacle or Temple of the Old Testament with its Ark). God personally will minister to them and care for them. All things will be made new!

The expression *"these words are faithful and true"* is significant! You can trust God! This is a message the persecuted saints needed to hear! Although their present life was full of suffering, in the new heaven God will personally be there to care for them!

The expression *"It is done!"* is interesting! It is similar yet different from Rev 16:17. Rev 16:7 in Greek is in the *third* person *singular*, *It is done*! Here in Rev 21:6 the Greek is in the *third* person *plural*, which should be translated *All things are done*! The expression at Rev 16:17 *"it is done"* stressed that Rome had been judged in answer to the saints' prayer of Rev 6:10! At Rev 21:6, *"all things are done"*, Rome, Satan, and all the wicked have been judged! *It's all over, the new heaven and new earth have arrived, the old earth has passed away, and the New Jerusalem has arrived! "Hallelujah!"*

Notice, nothing unclean enters this city, none of the cowardly and unfaithful who worshipped the beast and who had received his mark on their forehead may enter this city. Only the faithful martyrs and all the faithful of all ages can enter this city.

## The Glory of the Holy City, the New Jerusalem (Rev 21:9-14)

An angel, one of the seven who had the seven bowls of God's wrath explained that the city, the New Jerusalem, was inhabited by the Bride of the Lamb. At Rev 19 the Bride of the lamb was the saints who had conquered. The point is that the martyred saints may have been barred for Rome, but they are now to be found in the New Jerusalem!

The city has twelve gates with the names of the twelve tribes of Israel written on them. There are twelve gates with twelve angels guarding them. They represent the twelve tribes of Israel, God's people. The wall of the city has twelve foundations named after the twelve apostles, again symbolic of Christians. All of the faithful saints from both the Old Testament and Christian ages are represented and permitted to enter the city.

The twelve angels at the twelve gates permit no unclean person to enter the city. The unclean in the context of Revelation are those who have worshipped the beast!

## The Measurements of the City (Rev 21:15-18)

At Rev 11 God had John measure the temple. (Ezekiel had measured the Temple and city of ancient Jerusalem (Ezek 40:1ff). This symbolized that God knew who his people were. Now we encounter the New Jerusalem. It is measured and is enormous!

Again measuring the city implies that God knows all about the people of the city, for they are his people! And the number of his people is enormous. The saints are not alone!

## The Foundations of the City (Rev 21:19-21)

The foundations of the city are of the purest and best jewels. It is beautiful! The jewels are symbolic of the glory of the New Jerusalem which draws its beauty from the presence of God.

There are twelve gates to this city, each an enormous pearl! In ancient cities certain gates were reserved for certain people and purposes. The Shepherds Gate in Jerusalem was for shepherds! The repeated figure of twelve is in keeping with Revelation and the Jewish tradition of twelve tribes. The figure twelve is a symbol of God's people.

## The Light of the City (Rev 21:22-27)

Temples were a place where people could come into the presence of God. God "visited" the temple! In this city there is no need for a temple for God is there in person! Because God is present there is no need for sun and moon for God is their light.

People from all nations enter this city, *but* no one *unclean* may enter this city! Remember in the *context* of Revelation the *unclean* are those who have worshipped the beast (Rome). They uttered the lie, confessing that *"Caesar is Lord"*.

## The Sustenance of the City (Rev 2:1-5)

Those who *conquered* (Rev 2 and 3) had been offered by Jesus spiritual food, *the tree of life* (Rev 2:7), and *manna*. They had been promised a little white stone (Rev 2:17) which represented an invitation to the eschatological (end of the world) banquet with God and Jesus. John now describes the spiritual food of this New Jerusalem.

In this city is the river of the water of life. In Judaism the water of life represented God's sustaining power. In the wilderness God had provided water for Israel. Now in this New Jerusalem we find the source of this water!

This city has fruit for every occasion from the tree of life! Twelve kinds of fruit for each month of the year are on either side of the river. (Interestingly we encounter the figure twelve again!)

The key to this is that it is God's presence that sustains life completely!

Again John emphasizes that there will be nothing accursed in the city, only the throne of God, of the Lamb, and of those servants who worship God and the Lamb. In the context of Revelation, the churches in Asia, and the conflict with Rome, the accursed are those who worship the beast and receive his mark. They have no place in this city. The Greek word for accursed carries a significant meaning! Κατάθεμα, *katathema, something that has been delivered over to divine wrath,* an *accursed thing, anything accursed.*

In the broader Christian context, which is not on John's mind at this point, this city will include all the faithful saints of all time.

## The Epilogue (Rev 22:6-21)

As we noticed previously, in the chiastic structural outline of Revelation, the Prologue runs parallel to the Epilogue. The Epilogue will repeat the primary message of the Prologue (Rev 1:1-20). The Prologue, like that of the Gospel of John, sets boundaries for the theological themes to be developed later in the book or letter. We should now watch for the themes that are repeated in Rev 22:6-21 that are parallel in Rev 1:1-17. These repeated themes form an *inclusio* which functions like *parentheses* or *book ends* that hold the themes of the narrative together.

The Prologue stressed the following important points or themes which are echoed in the Epilogue:
- *These words are trustworthy and true* (Rev 1:1-3, Rev 22:6).

- The words are revealed to *angels* who pass them on to the saints (Rev 1:1, Rev 22:6).
- This is a revelation from God through Jesus *to show to his servants* of *things that must soon* (*shortly*, KJV) take place (Rev 1:1, Rev 22:6). Notice the emphasis on *soon*! (Revelation is primarily about *things that will soon take place* and not about the end of the world which is mentioned tangentially in Rev 20:11-15 to close the theodicy of Revelation).
- *For the time is near* (Rev 1:3 and Rev 22:10). There is a *crisis* about to break in on the churches in Asia (*time*, Greek *kairos, a significant time* or *crisis is near*, Greek *eggus, an eschatological term that stresses exaggerated imminence*).
- *Jesus is coming soon* (Rev 22:7) *bringing his recompense* (Rev 22:12). This is not the end of the world judgment but Jesus' coming on the churches in Asia if they do not repent, and on Rome. (Note that Jesus' *coming soon* on the churches in Rev 2 and 3 was *conditional*, based on their repentance. If they repented he would not come and judge them.)
- *God is the Alpha and Omega, the first and the last* (Rev 1:8, Rev 22:13).

John mentions t*hose who have washed their robes have the right to the tree of life (*Rev 22:14)*.* These are the *conquerors* or *martyrs*. Remember at Rev 2:7, the *conquerors* [martyrs] also received *the tree of life*.

Outside the New Jerusalem or heavenly city are the *dogs, sorcerers, fornicators, murderers, and idolaters*, that is, those who worship the beast (cf. Rev 22:15). The *lie* in Revelation refers to those who committed the ultimate lie confessing that *Caesar is Lord*. Those who commit fornication are those who were seduced by the harlot [Rome] and who worshiped at the Imperial image of the Emperor.

*Do not seal up the words of the prophecy* (Rev 22:10). The words of this prophesy, that is, Revelation, are not to be sealed up (remember Dan 8:26, 12:4, where Daniel was told to *seal up* his message for the time was not yet, meaning his message was for later times). The words of Revelation are not to be kept for a later time but needed to be read and heard by the Christians living in Asia at the close of the first century AD.

An invitation is given to the saints to *"come"* up into the city where they will join other *conquerors* or martyrs. This is reminiscent of Rev 2 and 3 which stressed that the conquerors would be fed and given the water of life without price [it cannot be bought with money]. The saints are invited to come and join Jesus in his eternal kingdom and reign! In one sense, this is a call for martyrdom!

There was at Rev 1:3 an urgent encouragement to *hear* the words of the prophecy. Remember the exhortation to *continually read aloud*, to *continually hear*, and to *continually keep* what is written in the message of Revelation. This exhortation added a sense of urgency to the reading of Revelation. This is repeated at Rev 22:7b. Now at Rev 22:18 there is a warning not to *add* or *take away* from *the words of the book of this prophecy*, that is, the book of Revelation.

As encouragement to the suffering saints Jesus promises *"I am coming soon"* to judge their enemies and *bring their recompense*. It is important to keep these *coming soon* statements in the context of Revelation and not see them as promises regarding the second coming, for *soon* means *soon* or *shortly* (KJV)!

## What We Learn From this Chapter and Rev 20

- Rev 20 brings the story of the persecution of the church by Rome to a head and symbolic conclusion; Satan is completely bound, limited, in his ability to seduce Rome and the nations. He is able to seduce other nations such as Gog and Magog who represent the resilience of evil and evil nations.
- However, Satan, the beast, and the false prophet are thrown into the lake of fire, Hell.

- In this chapter John gives us a glimpse of the final judgment in order to bring the theodicy of Revelation to a close.

## The Story of Revelation

- To the surprise of many, Revelation is not really about the end of the world!
- Rev 1:1-3 explains that Revelation is about things that must soon take place in the lives of the Christians in Asia. A crisis was about to break in on them. This was so serious that God sent a message through Jesus and John to the seven churches of Asia.
- Revelation was written to the churches in Asia in the 1st century AD in the context of burgeoning persecution, suffering, and even martyrdom.
- It includes a call to die faithfully to Jesus as *conquerors* or martyrs rather than to compromise faith with Satan and the worldly powers.
- Revelation's primary message was to the churches in the 1st century. However, its relevance remains today through the theological themes that we find highlighted in the book.
- In the big picture (the full story of the Old and New Testaments) all faithful saints have a home in the New Jerusalem or heavenly city of God, but that was not the story or theology of Revelation!
- Revelation is focused on the churches in Asia who were about to experience or enter a crisis of faith challenging their faithfulness to God and Jesus.
- The context is the oppression at the hands of the Jewish Synagogue, their pagan neighbors, and the Imperial Cult of the Roman Empire. The message to the churches was to not compromise their faith by confessing that Caesar is Lord, that is, a divine being or god!
- The theology of Revelation is about suffering faithfully through persecution and difficulties in the knowledge that God is in control, that in Jesus he has provided us the

victory over Satan and sin, and that he has prepared a home for us in heaven as a reward for our faithfulness.
- The overall story or theology of Revelation is about conquering Satan through faith in Jesus.
- *It is about Victory in Christ!*

## Theological Lessons and Principles We Learn for Today from Revelation

- Revelation is not about the end of the world. It was about a crisis that was soon to break in on the churches in Asia.
- It is a prophecy predicting suffering, persecution, and conquering Satan through an uncompromising faith in Jesus.
- This world under the influence of Satan is a rough and dangerous world, full of evil.
- Revelation has end of the world implications in that it informs us that our present decisions are judged by God with the end of the world significance.
- God warns us in advance that life will be filled with difficulties and suffering.
- Satan will do everything in his power to get us to compromise our faith in Jesus with the world.
- God is in control of his creation and world and will provide an escape from Satan and his power through Jesus.
- We are called to an uncompromising faith in Jesus. We must get our faith worked out and focused before crises strike!
- It is Jesus who must be the center of our faith, not the church, not Scripture, not doctrine, not good works.
- We must work through understanding the *Holiness*, *Sovereignty*, and *Righteousness* of God.
- We may be called to die for our faith in Jesus, but the reward for faithfulness far outweighs the cost.
- Satan and those who choose to take his side will be held accountable by God and judged by God in His time.

- God has an eternal plan and he is working that plan. We must be faithful and patient as God works his plan.

# Addendum I
# Lessons for Today from Revelation and Millennial Views

## Introduction

We begin by reviewing the major theological themes we can learn from Revelation that are relevant for today, for Revelation is as relevant today as it was in the 1$^{st}$ century of Christianity!

Following this we will look briefly at several millennial views that impact how we read Revelation:
- Chiliasm
- Premillennialism
- Dispensationalism
- Post millennialism
- Amillennialism

## The Theology and Relevance of Revelation

One reason Christians have difficulty making sense of Revelation and its mysterious visions and images is that they do not understand how this strange book written over 1900 years ago can have meaning or relevance today. One's ability to find contemporary relevance in Revelation will determine how seriously one takes this magnificent book, and how often one returns to it for encouragement and comfort. We will notice shortly that much of the difficulty experienced by Christians today in understanding Revelation is compounded by the fact that it is written in an apocalyptic genre whose origins and meaning are formulated in persecution and oppression, and whose symbols are remote to the western technological mind unfamiliar with persecution. It is unlikely that Christians living in the twenty first century in western nations dominated by a "Christian" or even a "Semi-Christian" mindset will have to endure the kind of radical persecution experienced in the first three centuries of Christianity. Because of this, much of the message of Revelation which is shrouded in its strange otherworldly apocalyptic genre will seem remote or mystifying to many Christians. On the other hand, it is certain that Christians will face sociological trauma, terminal illness, economic stress, and personal suffering. The question is, therefore, "What does Revelation say to Christians living in a twenty first century post-modern society, and how does it convey its message?"

The search for contemporary relevance in Revelation is compounded further by Premillennial and Dispensational theories which tend to shift the meaning of Revelation away from contemporary trauma and suffering to the end of the world and final judgment. Once this shift has been accomplished contemporary concerns over the "signs of the times," the second coming of Jesus, and the end of the world have been substituted for the indispensable historical and socio-religious context of the oppression and persecution of the seven churches in Asia and Revelation, and the underlying theological message of this great book.

It is easy for the serious student of Revelation to get caught up in the euphoria of apocalyptic study, combat mythology, and the literary genius of John, and lose sight of John's primary concern, namely, that Christians not succumb to the pressures of their often pagan culture, and consequently compromise their faith with their secular world. There is always the temptation to approach a book like Revelation from an academic standpoint. This is always a temptation when writing a commentary on such literature. We become so fascinated with the strange visions and otherworldly images that our curiosity drives us deeper into the fields of literary and historical criticism in our quest to understand this unusual and fascinating book. The challenge to "master" the mysteries can cloud our vision and obscure the real meaning and purpose of the book. Rudolf Bultmann and Karl Barth warned in the early twentieth century against an obsession to master the text rather than being mastered by the message of the text! This warning is surely appropriate in the case of Revelation. However, some attempt must be given to understanding the wonderful and challenging theological and literary nature of Revelation.

There will be times when all Christians will feel powerless before illness, suffering, personal problems, and death. Revelation speaks as clearly in such contexts today as it did to Christians facing persecution in the first century. John's message in Revelation encouraged Christians to lift their eyes from their oppressive present, and to elevate their horizons from the persecutions of culture and the power of Rome. Revelation encouraged Christians to see their hope, not in the powers of this world, but in the heavenly (or cosmic) world of God's divine power. Christians were encouraged to see beyond their present suffering and to take courage in and be confident in God's sovereign power over the schemes of Satan which God had already proven in Jesus death and resurrection.

Revelation challenges Christians today to have confidence in God's power to provide for them a secure future. The message of Revelation, then, is that in Christ God has provided an effectual victory over suffering and despair, and a pathway into a warm loving fellowship with He who sits on the heavenly throne. Revelation draws attention to a Trinitarian God whose loving concern is to nurture the lonely, the hurting, the disenfranchised, and those without hope. The same God who lovingly gave his own son to die for the world, and who through his Holy Spirit was able to raise that Son to a triumphant victory over Satan is able to transform present Christian oppression and suffering into a glorious victory over life's struggles, even death, and the power of Satan.

The *primary* message of Revelation, then, is simply that Christians can achieve a magnificent *victory in Christ* over the power of Satan and this world. Christians facing extreme trauma are encouraged to keep their faith in the God in whom they have put their trust, and never to compromise that faith, and to be reminded that in Christ *"we are more than conquerors through him who loved us..."* (Rom 8:37). Christians are encouraged to set their spiritual eyes on the *Holiness, Sovereignty,* and *Righteousness* of God and to realize in the presence of God that even the worst enemy is powerless.

In addition to the primary message to the seven churches of victory in Christ, several salient messages can be found in this great book. Principally, the message was that the seven churches should examine their faith before serious crises break in on them. *Times of crisis are not the time for building faith!* In such times faith needs to break through the crisis and sustain the believer. Christians are encouraged to build their faith before crises strike so that faith may be ready to sustain them in times of tragedy.

In addition, Revelation encourages Christians to seriously contemplate the *love and power* of God *while things are going reasonably well*. Prior to catastrophe striking, Christians need to have their faith fully informed in regard to the God in whom they believe. They need to clarify their understanding of the nature and character of the God of love and grace as a foundation to trials. When Christians understand the *sovereignty* of God; that *He* is in control of the universe, not Satan or anyone else, they are able to withstand Satan and his wiles. When Christians understand the *holiness* of God; that *He* is *wholly different* from everything sinful and weak, then Christians too can strive to be different (holy) from the world and their secular pagan culture. When Christians understand the *righteousness* of God, that *He never makes a mistake*, then they are able to see life from a different perspective and to work through the troubling times and disturbing questions that surface in the trials of life, understanding that God is greater than the trials that surround them. Passages such as Rev 4 in which John describes the magnificence, holiness, sovereignty, and righteousness of God are intended to encourage Christians to lift their eyes toward heaven and to contemplate the triumphant and all powerful God who is able to overcome all trials. Revelation does not attempt to deny the reality of persecution and oppression, but encourages Christians to see beyond these to a God who historically has been, and who continues to be able to transcend all human suffering. This God is the Almighty Lord of Hosts *who is, who was, and who is to come*. He never changes (Rev 1:4, 8)!

An equally important lesson to be learned from Revelation is that this God has eternally been concerned for his saints. He began planning in eternity for their needs well in advance of any future necessity, and he has been working that plan in history

(*Heilsgeschichte*) throughout the ages. A particular focus of this is seen in God's eternal plan that unfolds in breaking open the sealed scroll of Rev 5. This leads through seven trumpets in a dramatic progression toward the revelation of Jesus, the triumphant Lamb in Rev 12:10, 11 who has already conquered Satan and his power. This scroll and series of seals assures the saints that God has an eternal plan for his creation and that he has been working that plan. This plan focuses on or reaches its apex in the death and resurrection of Jesus. Christians are thus assured in Revelation of the constant abiding presence of this triumphant Jesus in the everyday events and struggles of life, for this Jesus walks constantly in the presence of his churches (lampstands), Rev 2:1.

The theology of Revelation, therefore, is that God is the loving sovereign of the universe. Although he hates sin and evil he tolerates it in his love for man but will eventually destroy evil and those associated with evil. Revelation admits that God understands his creation will suffer under the evil workings of Satan, but affirms that he has already provided an escape from Satan and the power of evil through the death and resurrection of Jesus. Revelation affirms that God will in the end, when his purpose is fulfilled, reach into the affairs of this world and judge and destroy Satan and those who follow him. In the meantime, those who endure faithfully are guaranteed that they will reign with Christ in his kingdom. Perhaps the climax of Revelation is found in the verses of Rev 12:10, 11, *"...Now the salvation (victory, IAF) and the power and the kingdom (reign, IAF) of our God and the authority of his Christ* have come, *for the accuser of our brethren* has been thrown down, *who accuses them day and night before our God. And they* have conquered *him by the blood of the Lamb and by the word of their testimony, for they loved not their lives even unto death."*

In the title to his commentary on Revelation, *More Than Conquerors*, William Hendriksen, caught the meaning and theology of Revelation. Hendriksen insightfully drew on that great passage in Rom 8:37 for the title of his book; *"who shall separate us from the love of Christ? Shall tribulation, or distress, or persecution, or famine, or nakedness, or peril, or sword? No, in all these things* we are more than conquerors *through him who loved us"!* Hence the title of this commentary, *Conquering in Christ!*

## Millennial Views

The following notes on Millennial Views are taken from my larger commentary on Revelation, *Conquering With Christ*.

Several models fall under the nomenclature of Millennialism or Millenarianism. All reflect in some measure an eschatological or futurist interpretation, each with its own peculiar characteristics. All millennial views are an attempt to explain the fascinating and challenging use of 1000 years in Rev 20 (*millennial* deriving from the Latin *mille*, meaning 1000). The first two to be considered, Premillennialism and Dispensationalism, are characterized by an extreme literal interpretation, particularly of Old Testament prophecy, and have a decided futurist inclination. The third group, Postmillennialism shares with Premillennialism and Dispensationalism only the fact that it is a form of millennial interpretation, albeit significantly different from the previous two. Both Premillennialism and Dispensationalism consider Rev 4-21 to deal exclusively with the final days of history. They are in that sense fully eschatological interpretations. We will look finally at Amillennialism, which although it shares with the above three views the term "millennialism," differs in that it does not break history into millennial dispensations, nor does it take 1000 years literally in reference to time. I will present a diagrammatic overview of the various millennial positions at the conclusion of this discussion.

## Chiliasm

The term Chiliast derives from the Greek *chilias* meaning "thousand." It is a term best reserved in Revelation studies for *ancient second and third century views* relating to the 1000 years of Rev 20. This brief survey of Chiliasm may be an oversimplification of Chiliasm and may do an injustice to some ancient Chiliast views. Nevertheless it will set out the main thrust of Chiliast thinking. Chiliasm is a futurist view that holds that Jesus will return to earth at the end of the church age and establish his kingdom of 1000 years. Most, but not all Chiliasts viewed this 1000 year reign as a literal reign on earth. There is some question among some as to whether the 1000 year reign should be interpreted literally or symbolically, or whether it will take place on earth or not. Since the prevailing biblical hermeneutic in the early years of Christian interpretation was overwhelmingly literalist in its method, Chiliasm reflected this literalist approach to Scripture. Suffice it to say that even today literalist views of Scripture generally accept the church age as *a form* of the kingdom of Jesus on earth, albeit in an imperfect stage, but that the *fulfilled* kingdom age is yet future. Chiliast's held that Christ had overcome Satan on the cross, but it would only be after his *parousia* (return, or second coming) that Satan would be finally destroyed and the kingdom on earth *fully* established. The point to notice at this stage is that the Chiliast *often equated the church age with the kingdom in some form* of reign of Christ, albeit one not yet *the fulfilled kingdom* on earth.

Since the early development of Chiliasm was at a time when the church was struggling to establish itself in a pagan culture the historical context of most Chiliast interpretations was one of the church harassed under persecution. Under these circumstances it can be understood why the Chiliast believed that Christ was already reigning in his kingdom but not yet fully in an earthly kingdom. It was apparent that although Christ was reigning in his spiritual kingdom, many on earth did not acknowledge his sovereignty. It would therefore be necessary according to the Chiliast view for Christ to return to earth to fully and finally establish his sovereignty and literally reign over all the earth.

We conclude that the Chiliast model is a form of futurist pre-millennial view in that it held that Christ must return to earth before he can literally and fully establish his 1000 year reign and kingdom. We should, however, not be hasty as are some Premillennialists (George Eldon Ladd for instance) to identify Chiliasm with Premillennialism, calling modern Premillennialism *Historic* Premillennialism, indicating that Premillennialism was the historic view of the second century church. There are similarities between Chiliasm and Premillennialism, but also notable differences. The major failure of the Chiliast and all premillennial futurist views is their excessive literalist interpretation of Scripture in which all texts are treated on the same level, thus ignoring the nature of symbolism and allegory in the various literary forms of Scripture, and a failure to keep the interpretation imbedded in the historical context of the churches in Asia in the 1st century.

## Premillennialism

In some senses, Premillennialism is very similar to Chiliasm. George Eldon Ladd argues his case for Historic Premillennialism (another way of defining Modern Premillennialism) from Chiliasm, maintaining that Historical (Modern) Premillennialism, with its roots in Chiliasm, and is therefore the oldest known form of Revelation hermeneutic. Modern Premillennialism, however, differs from ancient Chiliasm in that it separates more purposefully the church age from the kingdom age, and places significant emphasis on the final "signs of the times" which are anticipated immediately prior to the eschatological end of the world. Most Modern Premillennial views understand the church age to be a form of "spiritual" kingdom which has yet to be fulfilled. The fulfillment of the messianic kingdom will come only after the return of Jesus. Modern Premillennial interpretations vary considerably, manifesting a wide range of interests. A major claim of this group is that certain national prophecies made to Israel were not yet fulfilled, either in Israel or the church. These prophecies therefore remain to be fulfilled in a future kingdom of God to be established under Jesus on earth. Most Premillennial views identify Jerusalem as the place of that fulfillment. In some Premillennial programs the return of Jesus to establish his kingdom will be "triggered" by the rediscovery of the Ark of the Covenant. A major weakness of this method of interpretation is its literalist interpretation of Scripture and failure to give due course to the eschatology used by John in writing Revelation. In addition to George Eldon Ladd, one of the more competent, yet moderate, Premillennial interpreters in recent years has been G. R. Beasley-Murray (1974).

## Dispensationalism

Dispensationalism is an extreme form of Premillennialism. The origins of Dispensationalism can be traced to John Nelson Darby (1850), one of the founders of the Plymouth Brethren movement in Ireland. Darby was a well educated lawyer. Dissatisfied with his Church of England roots he separated from them over problems relating to allegiance to the King and State. Darby argued that the prophecies to Israel regarding the kingdom had not been fulfilled in the church age and remained yet to be fulfilled. In fact, Darby argued, the Old Testament is silent regarding the church! Darby's views eventually found their way to the United States.

A self-taught Bible student, successful American real estate businessman, and early leader in the American Christian Zionism movement, William E. Blackstone (1908) was impressed with Darby's literalist interpretation of Scripture and became a proponent of this view. Darby's dispensational views were also adopted by C. I. Schofield (of *The Schofield Reference Bible* fame, 1909). Schofield became a Presbyterian minister in Dallas, Texas. John Walvoord (1959) subsequently came under the influence of Schofield's Dispensational leanings. Through his teaching and writing, Walvoord became mentor to Hal Lindsey, who then popularized a Dispensational model through his best-selling work, *The Late Great Planet Earth* (1970). Dispensational views cut across most denominational lines and can be found in the Seventh Day Adventist Church (with William Miller of the 1840's a pioneer of this movement), The Church of Jesus Christ of Latter Day Saints (Joseph Smith, 1830, was the founder of this restoration and millennial movement), the Jehovah's Witnesses (founder, Charles Taze Russell, 1870), and the World Wide Church of God (founder Herbert W. Armstrong, 1933). The Dallas Theological Seminary (founder and first president, Dr. Lewis Sperry Chafer, 1924; and Dr. John Walvoord, professor and the second president, 1950's) has been a primary source of Dispensational theology since its inception. A popular contemporary pop-theology writer, Tim F. Lahaye, co-writer of the *Left Behind* series, reflects dispensational views.

Basic Dispensational views (and there are a variety of Dispensational interpretations) hold that God had *intended* to establish his kingdom under Jesus, but when the Jews rejected Jesus, God *postponed* his kingdom, and *stopped the prophetic clock*. Daniel 9 is a key passage for all Dispensational interpretation. At some time in the future, indicated to man by the "signs of the times," God would restart the clock and the final "week" of Daniel 9 would begin. The final "week" will be marked by seven years of tribulation, "rapture", and Jesus' second coming to establish his delayed kingdom on earth in Jerusalem. A "realized Jewish kingdom" and the Jewish system will be reestablished with the rebuilding of the Temple in Jerusalem.

Clarence B. Bass, *Backgrounds to Dispensationalism*, while tracing the origins of Dispensationalism back to Darby, summarizes the basic tenets of this model of interpreting Revelation and the Bible as follows:

> What, then, are the distinguishing features of dispensationalism? They are: its view of the nature and purpose of a dispensation; a rigid applied literalism in the interpretation of Scripture; a dichotomy between Israel and the church; a restricted view of the church; a Jewish concept of the kingdom; a postponement of the kingdom; a distinction between law and grace that creates a multiple basis for God's dealing with man; its view of the purpose of the great tribulation; its view of the nature of the millennial reign of Christ; its view of the eternal state, and its view of the apostate nature of Christendom.

The major objection we have to this system is its radical literal interpretation of Scripture, the restoration of the Jewish Temple and sacrificial system, and the radical speculation and timetable of history triggered by every war or uprising in the Middle-East. Furthermore, this system like other futurist eschatological models removes the message of Revelation from those for whom the book was originally written and who urgently needed comfort and encouragement. There is little encouragement held out for the persecuted first century church in the Dispensational hermeneutic of Revelation!

## Postmillennialism

Postmillennialism was initially popularized by Daniel Whitby (1638-1726), a Unitarian minister in England. As Postmillennialism has developed since Whitby, the basic proposition of postmillennial thinking is that the 1000 years is not necessarily a literal time period but is symbolic of an age of great religious optimism and awakening in which the kingdom of God is extended in the world through the preaching of the gospel and the saving work of the Holy Spirit. It holds that the world is getting better and will eventually be "Christianized". The return of Christ will follow the Christianization of the world. The Christianized period is therefore referred to as the millennium. The view is highly optimistic to say the least, and is fundamentally more sociologically motivated than biblically grounded!

Postmillennialism became popular in America in the late eighteenth and early nineteenth centuries. The optimism of the time, however, was dealt a serious blow by the American Civil War which could hardly be considered as a harbinger of the spread of the gospel of peace! Such was the optimism and confidence of postmillennialists in the nineteenth century that the movement was not unduly set back by these events. Alexander Campbell, a prominent leader of the Restoration Movement and Churches of Christ in America in the nineteenth century was a staunch supporter and proponent of Postmillennialism. Campbell and Barton W. Stone, another prominent leader among Churches of Christ, had read a book by Elias Smith on Postmillennialism and fully accepted Smith's view. Campbell developed and popularized his postmillennial thoughts through his religious journal *The Millennial Harbinger*. In later years Moses Lard and T. W. Brents of the same Restoration Movement turned away from Campbell's Postmillennialism and introduced a form of chiliast pre-millennialism. Brents had learned of chiliasm from reading John Albrecht Bengel, *Gnomon Novi Testamenti*, (1752) in which Bengel revived a form of ancient Chiliasm. Other nineteenth century American postmillennialists were Charles Hodge, David Brown, and B. B. Warfield. More recent postmillennialists are Loraine Boettner and Marcellus Kik. The major problems encountered in Postmillennialism are first, the doctrine is simply not biblically supported, and second, Postmillennialism is sociologically naive.

## Amillennialism

Amillennial scholars draw heavily on both the Moderate Preterist and Philosophy of History schools of thought. They do not see in the 1000 years a *literal* reference to a *time period*. Amillennialism is thus opposed to a millennial interpretation that fixates on a *period of time*. Hence, it is a-millennial, or not-millennial! The term amillennial derives from the *alpha privative "a"* (a negative meaning *not*) and the word *"millennial"*. It defines a concept that claims to not be Millennial in thinking!

The Amillennial approach to Revelation is sensitive to historical, sociological, literary, and reader response critical concerns which recognize that Revelation is a highly theological symbolic work in a unique apocalyptic and eschatological genre. Amillennial thinkers are also sensitive to the heightened dramatic element in Revelation. Most Amillennial scholars can, therefore, be subsumed under either the Moderate Preterist or Philosophy of History groups. The Amillennial "school", because of its responsive mindset to the full range of Biblical hermeneutics, is "allergic" to literalist approaches to Revelation! Reluctant to interpret the high symbolism and apocalypticism of Revelation literally, the Amillennialist sees in the numerical symbolism of Revelation theological rather than literal or temporal references. Amillennialism perceives the 1000 year reign of the saints with Christ to be *symbolic*, not of temporal concerns, but of the *extent* and *completeness* of the reign of martyrs who have died for their witness to Christ. Amillennialists do not understand the millennium to be a *period* of time, but find in it a *set of conditions* symbolically depicted by a 1000 years. They consider Revelation to be set in the context of the first century Church struggling to be faithful to God and Christ in a pagan world that does not understand its Christian commitment. Amillennialists consider the theology of Revelation to confirm that death (martyrdom) for Christ is not defeat, but a sacrifice that results in a resounding personal victory in Christ. Those who die for (and with) Christ as martyrs reign with him *completely* (symbolized by 1000 years, 1000 symbolizing completeness). This commentary is written out of a Moderate Preterist model combined with a Philosophy of History sensitivity that results in an Amillennial perspective. Amillennialist commentators lean heavily on an historical and literary critical analysis of Revelation.

# Addendum II
# The Chiastic Structure of Revelation

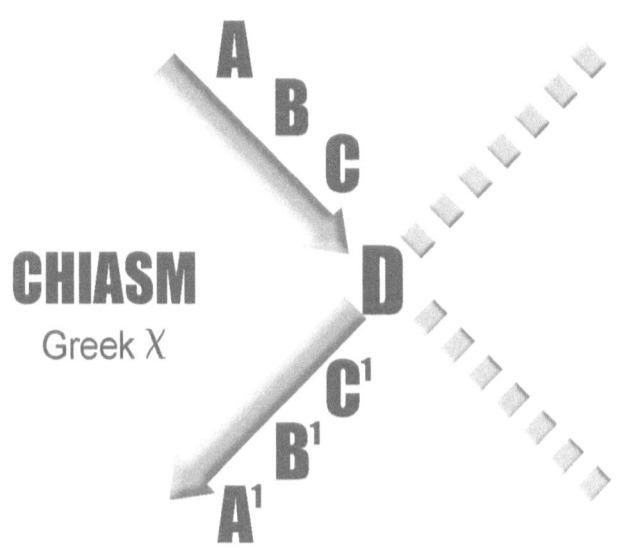

Prologue 1:1-20
I. The Church in Imperfection. 2:1-3:22
   Seven Letters to the Seven Churches
    II. The Authority of God over Evil Explained. 4:1-8:6
      Seven Seals on the Scroll
      III. The Warning Judgments. 8:1-11:19
         Seven Trumpets
         IV. The Lamb - God's Answer to Evil. 12:1-14:20
           Seven Unnumbered Figures
      V. The Consummated Judgments. 15:1-16:21
         Seven Bowls of Wrath
    VI. The Authority of God over Evil Exercised. 17:1-20:15
      Seven Unnumbered Descriptions of God's Judgments
VII. The Church in Perfection. 21:1-22:5
   Seven Unnumbered Descriptions of the Church in Perfection
Epilogue 22:6-21

# NOTES:

1. Note that the climax or high point in this chiastic structure is *The Lamb – God's answer to evil*.
2. The *Prologue* and *Epilogue* are primarily parallel in language and content.
3. Points I. and VII. are parallel:
   Points II. and VI. are parallel:
   Points III. and V. are parallel.

# Addendum III

# The Story of Revelation

## The Context

1. Historical:
   a. 1st cent A.D. churches in the Roman Province of Asia.
   b. Impending Roman Persecution – Rev 1:1-3: "Things that must soon take place…for the time is near (imminent).
   c. There is a war going on between God and his agents (the church) and Satan and his agents (Rome, the Synagogue, and Paganism).
2. Literary:
   a. Revelation is a theological drama set in two major acts; Act 1: Rev 1-11; Act 2: Rev 12-22.
   b. The visions and scenes are not time sequential but are a repetitive rebirth of images and visions in a kaleidoscopic manner.
   c. Old Testament: Dan 7; Ezek 1:1-3:3; Psalm 2; Zechariah; Isaiah; Jeremiah; et al.
   d. Pseudepigrapha; Apocrypha; apocalyptic tradition; *Tobit*, *Sib. Oracles*; et al.
3. Theological:
   a. Roman Imperial Cult idolatry; Faithfulness to Jesus; No compromise.
   b. Martyrdom is victory over Satan, conquering (overcoming in NIV).
   c. The saints have already conquered Satan by their faithfulness, martyrdom, and the blood (death, martyrdom) of Jesus Rev 12:10.
   d. Martyrdom is interpreted by John as a sacrifice to God.
   e. The martyred saints are a kingdom of priests whose reward for faithfulness is eternal life with God and reigning with Jesus on his throne.

    f. The eschatological framework (*eschatos*, last days, Christian kingdom age) is that God has already judged Satan, Rome, and evil with end of the world judgment which he pronounces in advancer in final end of the world language and significance (proleptic eschatological pronouncements).
4. Theodicy:
    a. God is a Holy; Sovereign; Righteous God
    b. He has a plan (*Heilsgeschichte* and the Scroll of Rev 5, 6) for taking care of evil and has already begun this plan at the cross of Jesus.
5. The Antagonist:
    a. Satan; Civil power of Rome; Imperial Cult; Paganism; the Synagogue; those who dwell on the earth who worship the beast.
6. The Protagonist:
    a. The Eternal God; The Son; The Holy Spirit; Michael and the angels.

## The Story

**Rev 1:** The Prologue
    The Message from God to the churches in Asia – "things that must soon take place, the crisis time is near".
    The Greeting – From the whole Godhead.
    John is instructed by Jesus to write letters to the seven churches of Asia

**Rev 2, 3:** The seven letters to the seven churches calling on them to get their faith sorted out and focused on Jesus.

**Rev 4:** The heavenly throne room scene with God on his throne surrounded by the four living creatures and 24 martyr representative elders.

**Rev 5:** the large scroll sealed with seven seals – God's plan (Heilsgeschichte) for dealing with the problem of evil.

**Rev 6:** The beginning of opening the seven seals. 6:10 is important – the prayers of the martyred saints for vindication; they are told to wait for a while as God works his plan.

**Rev 7:** The Interlude of God sealing the 144,000, his church militant. The listing of the 12 tribes of Israel is highly symbolic.

**Rev 8-9:** The seven warning trumpets against Rome, calling on evil persons to repent.

**Rev 10, 11:** The second Interlude, John told to eat the small scroll which contains a bitter and sweet message. He is told he must preach the message again. The measuring of the temple representing God's people, and not measuring the outer court which represents those who compromise their faith and worship the beast.

**Rev 12:** The two messianic communities, the war in heaven between Michael and Satan, the defeat of Satan, the hymn of rejoicing that the martyred saints have already conquered Satan by their faith and the blood (death) of the lamb, Jesus.

**Rev 13:** The two evil beasts, Leviathan (civil power of Rome) and Behemoth (the Imperial cult – the religious side of Rome). The beasts make war on the Saints. Those who dwell on earth (who worship the beast) receive the mark of the beast, 666, which is a human number in contrast to Jesus' number, 888 (the Sibylline Oracles).

**Rev 14:** The Lamb reigning on Mount Zion (Ps 2) with the 144,000 martyred saints who represent the church victorious. Seven angelic messages calling for repentance and warning of judgment on Babylon (Rome).

**Rev 15:** Return to the Throne Room of God with praise of God for exercising his sovereign power. Seven final bowls of plagues to be poured out on Rome representing God's final judgment on Rome.

**Rev 16:** The seven bowls of God's judgment poured out on Babylon Rome). The Battle of Armageddon (*Har Megiddo*) symbolic of God's great victory over the enemy. (Remember the symbolism of Waterloo, and Dec 7, The Alamo!)

**Rev 17:** The Great harlot, (Rome), and the Seven and eighth kings who all go on to perdition (judgment and ruin).

**Rev 18, 19:** The doom of Babylon (symbolic of God's judgment on Rome). The beast (the Civil power of Rome) and the false prophet (the Imperial cult) cast into the lake of fire, hell!

**Rev 20:** The complete (1,000 years) binding of Satan (Limitation of Satan's ability to use Rome). The full reign of the saints with Christ (1,000 years completeness). This is not on earth! The final judgment of Satan (the devil) and cast into the lake of fire where the beast (Civil power of Rome) and the false prophet (the Imperial cult) are already judged.

**Rev 21:** The New Heaven and New Earth where God lives with his triumphant church. The sea (the source of evil) is no more, Satan has gone! All things are done, God's plan is completed!

**Rev 22:** The Epilogue, repeats the theme of the Prologue.

# Glossary of Terms

## Bibliography

The following definitions of key expressions in Revelation studies is adapted from several reference works, among them: John J. Collins, *The Apocalyptic Imagination: An Introduction to the Jewish Matrix of Christianity*, (New York: The Crossroad Publishing Company, 1984), John J. Collins, Ed., *Apocalypse: The Morphology of a Genre* (Semeia 14: The Society of Biblical Literature, 1979), Everett Ferguson, Editor, *Encyclopedia of Early Christianity*, (New York: Garland Publishing Co., 1990), Paul D. Hanson, *The Dawn of Apocalyptic* (Philadelphia: The Fortress Press, 1975), and Richard N. Soulen, *Handbook of Biblical Criticism* (Atlanta: John Knox Press, 1981), *The Anchor Bible Dictionary* (New York: Doubleday, 1992), *The International Standard Bible Encyclopedia*, (Michigan: Wm. B. Eerdmans, 1979), M. R. James, *The Apocryphal New Testament*, (Oxford: Claredon Press, 1950), Edgar Hennecke and William Schneemelcher, *New Testament Apocrypha*, 2 Vols., (Philadelphia: the Westminster Press, 1963), James M. Robinson, *The Nag Hammadi Library in English*, (San Francisco: Harper, 1990), Edgar J. Goodspeed, *The Apocrypha: An American Translation*, (Chicago, Ill.: University of Chicago Press, 1938), Edgar J. Goodspeed, *The Story of the Apocrypha*, (Chicago, Ill.: University of Chicago Press, 1939), G. W. E Nickelsburg, *Jewish Literature Between the Bible and the Mishna*, (Philadelphia: Fortress Press, 1981), M. Stone, *Jewish Writings of the Second Temple Period*, (Philadelphia: Fortress Press, 1984), and Robert G. Clouse, Ed., *The Meaning of the Millennium: Four Views*, (Downers Grove: InterVarsity Press, 1977.)

## Amillennialism

Amillennialism is one of the terms used to describe theological theories regarding the 1000 year reign or the "anticipated" millennial reign of Christ. Other terms falling under the category of millennial theology are Premillennialism,

Dispensationalism, and Postmillennialism. Each of these is discussed in its own right in the glossary.

As will be noticed under the discussion of Millennialism, the term derives from the Latin terminology for 1000 years, namely, *mille* – 1000, and *annus* – year. Hence the term millennial refers to theories of the 1000 year reign of Christ of Rev 20:4.

Amillennial is the term used to refer to theories that do not see in Rev 20:4 and the 1000 years a literal period of time, or to that extent, any period of time. Amillennial theories suggest that the millennium refers rather to conditions or situations implying *completeness*, since the figure 1000 is understood to refer to completeness. In the case of Rev 20:4 the reign of the martyrs for 1000 years refers to the fact that they reign *completely* with Christ. They are conquerors (victorious) and thus share with Christ in his victory and reign. Rev 20:4 does not say that Christ reigns for 1000 years, or that his reign is on earth. It is the martyrs who reign *completely* with Christ (for 1000 years with the 1000 figuratively referring to the completeness of their reign).

Amillennial theories do not follow a literal interpretation of the figurative language of apocalyptic and Revelation, and furthermore are committed to setting the message of Revelation within the context of the $1^{st}$ century church suffering under Roman persecution. Amillennial scholars explain that the theological principles revealed in the message of Revelation to the $1^{st}$ century church apply today to Christians suffering persecution or affliction.

## Antichrist

The term "antichrist" nowhere appears in the text of Revelation itself, but is found often in commentaries, especially those coming from some Protestant, Fundamentalist, or Dispensationalist persuasions. The Greek term *antichristos* appears only five times in the New Testament, and only in the Johannine Epistles (1 Jn 2:18, 22; 4:3; and 2 Jn 7). In the Johannine Epistles the term is used only in regard to those who deny that Jesus is the Christ or that Jesus Christ came in the flesh. In this case the problem seems to be a Gnostic type heresy (see

Glossary under Gnosticism) which in no way addresses the theological problem of Revelation. The use of the term "antichrist" in the context of Revelation is unfortunate, arising in most cases from a poor understanding of who the beast is in Revelation, and the nature of the problem Christians were encountering with the beast. This commentary will not make reference to the "antichrist" nor refer to the beast as the antichrist. Certainly, the beast is opposed to the Christian faith and in that sense is anti-Christian, but the term "antichrist," having been used in the biblical text in other contexts, is not suitable for this study.

## Apocalyptic

Apocalyptic derives from the Greek word *apokalypsis* meaning "a revelation, an uncovering, or a disclosure." Apocalyptic is a broad term, appearing first in Biblical criticism at the beginning of the 19th cent. The term is used to designate those ancient visionary writings or parts of writings which, like the NT apocalypse from which the name is derived, namely, the book of Revelation, claim to reveal mysteries relating to the end of the world (age) and the glories of a future transcendent world (age) that is to break into human experience.

Apocalyptic literature is not, however, limited to the canonical Scriptures, for a vast pool of apocalyptic, or heavily apocalyptically flavored texts are available to the biblical critic. This rich storehouse of information provided an appropriate and powerful vehicle for the authors of our biblical texts. This is particularly true of the author of Revelation who found in the apocalyptic mindset, genre, and literature a most suitable medium for his theological message.

The term is used in a variety of ways and may refer to a range of concepts and theological motifs typical of this genre of literature. It may refer to a sociological or theological mind set, a method of communicating, or a type (genre) of literature, all of which are heavily influenced by visions, symbols, cosmic eruptions and wars, and threatening beasts. Biblical apocalyptic is a distinctive Jewish and Christian phenomenon that flourished in the four centuries between 200 B.C. and 200 A.D. the roots of apocalyptic, however, reach back into the 6th and 5th cent. B.C. Two of the best examples of the Biblical genre are Daniel and the book of Revelation. Many other Biblical texts, both Old and New Testament draw in varying degrees on the apocalyptic genre: Isa 13:4-16; 24-27 (the "Isaiah Apocalypse"); Joel 2; Zech 9-11, 12-14; Ezek 38-39; Amos 5:16-20; 9:11-15; Mk 13; Mat 23-25; Lk 21; 1 Thess 4-5; 2 Thess 2:1-2; 1 Cor 15; Rom 1:18-32; 8:18-25.

Many of the Pseudepigraphal and Apocryphal writings (see the glossary on these terms) are designated Apocalypses, or are considered to be heavily influenced by apocalyptic. Though no complete agreement exists, those so designated usually include: Apocalypse of Abraham; Apocalypse of Baruch (II or Syriac Baruch); Apocalypse of Esdras (IV Ezra 3-14); I Enoch; Book of Elijah; I Baruch; Apocalypse of Moses (or the Life of Adam and Eve); Apocalypse of Sedrach; Apocalypse of Elijah; II Enoch; Assumption of Moses; Sibylline Oracles; Book of Jubilees; Testament of Abraham; Testament of the Twelve Patriarchs; Ascension of Isaiah, et. al. Of this list, the first four, plus the canonical apocalyptically influenced Daniel and Revelation, are the best literary examples of this type.

Several of the Dead Sea Scrolls are also considered to be significantly influenced by apocalyptic interests. In particular the War Scroll, the Description of the New Jerusalem, and the Thanksgiving Psalms manifest striking apocalyptic features. Several prominent apocalyptic works found among the Dead Sea Scrolls indicate the apocalyptic interests of the Dead Sea Covenanters. They are Daniel; I Enoch; and Jubilees.

Challenging questions arise when discussing Apocalyptic: How does one define Apocalyptic? What are its unique characteristics? How does it work, and what was its purpose? What unique sociological and religious contexts gave rise to this genre? And why was it so popular among Jewish and Christian writers during the 400 years of its zenith? Several challenging questions have challenged scholars addressing this unique and fascinating genre. Questions as to whether it constitutes an identifiable literary genre continue to be debated, although an Apocalyptic Group meeting as part of the Society of Biblical

Studies study groups has made significant strides in identifying this genre. (See J. J. Collins' two works referenced below in the Bibliography.) Those with somewhat negative attitudes toward an identifiable literary genre argue that apocalyptic simply uses, adapts, and transforms older traditional genres. Klaus Koch has, however, identified six general literary features which are normally present in apocalypses: 1) discourse cycles (frequently called "visions") between the apocalyptic seer and a heavenly being, revealing the secret of man's destiny; 2) formalized phraseology depicting the spiritual turmoil of the seer (trance, etc.) that accompanies the vision; 3) a paraenetic discourse conveying an eschatological ethic or an introductory legend illustrating proper behavior; 4) pseudonymity, bearing the name of some ancient worthy - although the book of Revelation is an exception; 5) mythical images rich in symbolism (animals, angels, demons, cosmic phenomena); and, 6) a composite character (70 percent of the book of Revelation is influenced significantly by previously written sources).

In terms of general content, apocalyptic is characterized by the belief 1) that the radical transcendent transformation of this world lies in the immediate future (Dan 12:11,12; Rev 22:20; II Baruch 85:10; IV Ezra 4:50; 2) that a cosmic catastrophe (war, fire, earthquake, famine, pestilence) precedes the end; 3) that the epochs of history leading up to the end are predetermined; 4) that a hierarchy of angels and demons mediate the events in the two worlds (this world and the one to come) and that victory is assured to the divine realm; 5) that a righteous remnant will enjoy the fruits of salvation in a heavenly Jerusalem; 6) that the act inaugurating the kingdom of God and marking the end of the present age is His (or the Son of Man's) ascension to the heavenly throne; 7) that the actual establishment of the New Kingdom is effected through a royal mediator, such as the Messiah or the Son of Man, or simply and angel; 8) that the bliss to be enjoyed by the righteous can only be described as glory (Rev 21:1; Dan 12:3; I Enoch 50:1; etc.).

The origin of apocalyptic is variously ascribed to Hebrew prophecy, Iranian religion, Hellenistic syncretism, and Old Canaanite myths, with the greater number of scholars acknowledging at least the influence of eastern religion, particularly Zoroastrianism. For a full appraisal of the question of the origins of apocalyptic and the methodology used to answer it, see Paul D. Hanson, John J. Collins in the Bibliography below. Points often debated in contemporary NT scholarship relate to what extent Jesus and the NT writers, especially Paul, were influenced by apocalyptic; to what extent was apocalyptic pessimistic about world history; and to what extent can the kingdom of God be continuous with this world or the present age or time.

John J. Collins and his working associates in the apocalyptic study group propose the following working definition of an apocalypse: "Specifically, an apocalypse is defined as: *'a genre of revelatory literature with a narrative framework, in which a revelation is mediated by an otherworldly being to a human recipient, disclosing a transcending reality which is both temporal, insofar as it envisages eschatological salvation, and spatial insofar as it involves another, supernatural world.'"*

For the purpose of this study we will consider apocalyptic to be a mindset that expressed itself in literary form which eventually became an identifiable literary genre. The context of apocalyptic usually is a people under severe sociological, political, or religious opposition and persecution. Fundamentally pessimistic about human potential and the role of history (man's effort) to resolve the problem, apocalyptic looks to divine or transcendent intervention as the only hope for the future. Drawing on cosmic visions in a kaleidoscopic manner, and an intense symbolism, the author paints impressionistic pictures as he develops his theme. The primary theme or theology of apocalyptic, especially as it relates to the biblical texts and in particular, Revelation, is that the only hope for victory over the "enemy" is God's transcendent intervention. The persecuted are encouraged through the apocalyptic genre and its theology to not lose or compromise their faith, to be faithful to God "even unto death," and God would transform any defeat into a magnificent victory. In the words of Paul (Rom 8:37 ff) "we are more than conquerors through him who loved us." A major theme in Revelation is that Christians conquer Satan and the "enemy" through dying for their faith (martyr from the Greek *martus* mean to "witness to one's faith"). Martyrs are raised by the power of

God, thus vindicated by God, and reign with Christ in God's kingdom.

## Apocrypha

The term Apocrypha derives from the Greek *apokruphos* meaning "hidden' or "concealed." In biblical studies it has reference to a collection of writings that are considered highly spiritual, close to the biblical mindset, yet not completely in keeping with the biblical integrity. As a result the apocryphal books of Judaism and Christianity were not included in the biblical canon (list of books received by the church or community of faith as authoritative and normative. There are both New and Old Testament apocryphal books. Although not considered "inspired" or "normative" these writings were highly esteemed at the time the New Testament books were being produced and in many cases formed the conceptual framework of the writer. We will notice this in particular in regard to Revelation, but an interesting demonstration of this can be found in Jude 8, 9, 14. The Apocrypha became a plentiful and significant resource of ideas and expressions for the writer of Revelation.

## NT Apocrypha

The NT Apocrypha date from the second to the sixth centuries A.D. They are written in the form of gospels, acts, (histories), epistles, and apocalypses, and claim to report events, teachings, and prophecies related to Jesus and the early apostles which are not recorded in the canonical Scriptures. These writings contain little of historical value in terms of the subjects with which they deal (e.g., the birth of Mary, and the childhood of Jesus, etc.) but are of inestimable value in understanding the mind set of both orthodox and heterodox Christianity of the early centuries. Like the books of the NT, the apocryphal NT writings derive from the life and concerns of the early Christian communities.

The great flood of new material that in recent years has enriched the field of biblical studies, much of it due to the discovery in 1945 of a hoard of Coptic Gnostic texts at Nag in upper Egypt, has increased and enhanced the apocryphal materials available to scholars, and provided both a sociological and religious laboratory for research into early Christian beliefs and practices.

The following list of the most important apocryphal texts, organized into the four traditional categories represented in the canonical NT, demonstrates the proportions of this valuable resource of pseudo-biblical material:

***Gospels***: Arabic Gospel of the Infancy; Armenian Gospel of the Infancy; Assumption of the Virgin; Gospel of Bartholomew; the Book of the Resurrection of Christ by Bartholomew; gospel of Basilides; Gospel of Cerinthus; Gospel of the Ebionites; Gospel According to the Hebrews; Protoevangelium of James; History of Joseph the Carpenter; Gospel of Marcion; Gospel of the Birth of Mary; Gospel of Philip; Gospel of Pseudo-Matthew; and finally possible one of the most valuable, Gospel of Thomas.

***Acts***: Apostolic History of Abdias; Acts of Andrew; fragmentary story of Andrew; Acts of Andrew and Matthias; Acts of Andrew and Paul; Acts of Barnabas; Ascent of James; Acts of James the Great; Acts of John; Acts of John by Prochorus; Martyrdom of Matthew; Acts of Paul; Passion of Paul; Acts of Peter; Acts of Peter and Andrew; Acts of Peter and Paul; Acts of Philip; Acts of Pilate; Acts of Thaddaeus; Acts of Thomas.

***Epistles***: Epistles of Christ and Abgarus; Epistle of the Apostles; Third Epistle of the Corinthians; Epistle of the Laodiceans; Epistle of Lentulus; Epistles of Paul and Seneca; Apocryphal Epistle of Titus.

***Apocalypses***: Apocalypse of James; Apocalypse of Paul; Apocalypse of Peter; Revelation of Stephen; Apocalypse of Thomas; Apocalypse of the Virgin.

Additional writings, known by little more than their name, could be included in this list of Apocryphal writings, as well as some literature classified under other categories of early Christian literature.

## Old Testament Apocrypha

The OT Apocrypha is comprised of those books, or portions of books, included in the LXX (*Septuagint*, or Greek translation of the Hebrew Old Testament. Tradition has it that this translation was made in Alexandria, Egypt, in *circa* 270 B.C.), or included in the Old Latin translation of the LXX, but *not included in the Hebrew canon of the Old Testament*. These writings were accepted by some sectors of the early church as sacred writings, but were never included in the Hebrew canon. They represent deeply religious writings that date from *circa* 300 B.C. Some of them are as late as 70 A.D.

In preparing his edition of the Bible in Latin (known as the Vulgate), Jerome (*circa* 400 A.D.) chose to follow the Hebrew canon rather than the LXX which included the additional non-canonical books. Jerome included the additional books into a distinct corpus which he termed "apocryphal." These he also described as "ecclesiastical books" in contradistinction to the "canonical books" of the Hebrew OT. Since Jerome, the theological and physical place of the Apocrypha in the Christian canon has continued to be a matter of dispute, with the Eastern and Russian Orthodox, the Roman Catholics, and the Protestants accepting differing solutions as indicated below.

*Apocryphal books include:*

(A) Tobit; Judith; the Wisdom of Solomon; and Ecclesiasticus or the Wisdom of Jesus; the Son of Sirach - of the Apocrypha these alone were accepted as canonical by the Eastern Church at the Synod of Jerusalem in 1672.

(B) Baruch; the Letter of Jeremiah (or Baruch, ch. 6. In the LXX these two writings appear as additions to the book of Jeremiah); the Prayer of Azariah and the Song of the Three Young Men (or Holy Children); the History of Susanna, and Bel and the Dragon (in the LXX the last three appear as additions to the book of Daniel); and 1 and 2 Maccabees.

These writings, plus (A) above, were confirmed as canonical by the Council of Trent in 1548, though entitled "Deuterocanonical" since they did not appear in the Hebrew Bible.

(C) I Esdras (called Esdras A in the LXX, III Esdras in the Vulgate where Ezra and Nehemiah are called I & II Esdras) which contains portions of II Chron, Ezra, and Nehemiah plus other material; 2 Esdras (called IV Esdras in the Vulgate, also known as "The Ezra Apocalypse" (spec. Chs. 3-14), chs. 15-16 which are called V Esdras in some MSS [manuscripts] are a composite work and do not appear in the LXX); and, the Prayer of Manasseh, a brief penitential prayer - these writings were not confirmed as canonical by the Council of Trent and consequently appear in Catholic Bibles in an appendix or not at all (so the Jerusalem Bible). In modern Protestant editions of the Apocrypha (RSV, NEB) all of the above (A-C) are included.

(D) In the LXX and in the Appendix to the Greek canon one finds also Ps 151 and III & IV Maccabees.

## Chiasm

Chiasm is a technical term used in literary criticism and biblical interpretation to refer to a literary style or structure adopted by an author to add sequence, meaning, or force to the message. The background of the term chiasm is the Greek letter *chi* which when in written form is similar to the Arabic X. The front half of the X becomes the shape of the literary structure as indicated below in solid lines.

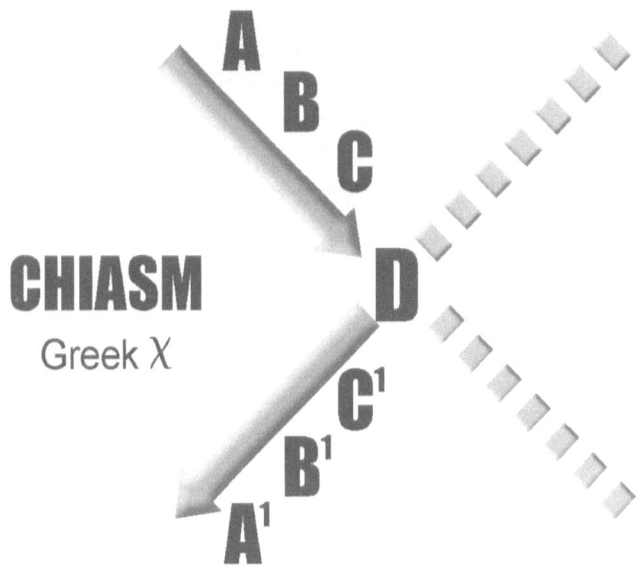

> The schematic of chiasm is that a statement is made (A) which is followed by a statement (B) which leads to the climactic statement (C). This is followed by another statement (B1), which is either parallel to (B) or antithetic to (B). A final statement (A1) follows which like (B1) is either parallel or antithetic to (A). By writing in this form the author builds an argument leading up to a climactic or main point.

It is the opinion of many scholars that the literary structure of Revelation is best described as a chiastic one in which the high point of the literary piece is Rev 12 and Christ the Lamb of God. This is more fully described in the Introduction to this study.

# Chiliasm

Like Millennialism, the term Chiliasm describes kingdom views relating to the 1000 year reign suggested in Rev 20:4-7. Chiliasm derives from the Greek word *chilias* meaning 1000. Chiliasm is the term used to describe 1st century views of the millennium. There are several similarities between Chiliasm and Premillennialism. An important difference between the two words Chiliasm and Millennialism is that the former is used almost exclusively for early 1st through 6th century theories relating to the 1000 year reign, whereas millennialism is used in reference to modern day theories. Because of the similarity of these two terms and their concepts, those like Eldon Ladd who espouse a form of Premillennialism known as Historic Premillennialism trace the roots of Premillennialism back to the 1st century Chiliasm. In fact, chiliasm *is* a form of premillennial thinking. As will be discussed below there are, however, significant differences between Chiliasm and Historic Premillennialism.

It seems that Chiliastic views had their roots in Phrygia in western Asia Minor, now Turkey. The general sense of chiliasm is that following the death and resurrection of Jesus the church was established in what one could term the church age. Due to early persecutions and social opposition the many Christians hoped for a future period of peace in which they, together with Christ, would reign in a peaceful kingdom. Such hopes gendered heated discussion and led to considerable controversy in the early church with opinions divided over whether this future kingdom would be physically on earth, or a spiritual kingdom in heaven. Because of this debate, some groups were reluctant to include Revelation in their canon since it was the source of much of this speculative theology. Primarily Chiliastic views were that with the second coming of Christ a kingdom would be established when the saints would be caught up to be with the Lord in his kingdom.

As one surveys Chiliastic views during the first six centuries one finds a wide range of ideas. Fundamental to all of them, however, is the longing for a period of peace following times of stress. Some views stressed that this 1000 year reign would be centered in Jerusalem and would be followed by the general resurrection and judgment. Chiliastic thought can be found in such early prominent figures as Papias, Bishop of Hierapolis (western Asia Minor), Justin Martyr, Hippolytus of Rome, Irenaeus, Bishop of Lyons, Methodius of Olympus, and others. Both Origen of Alexandria and Caesarea, and Augustine of Rome were staunch opponents of Chiliasm, preferring to see in the 1000 year reign a figurative symbol rather than a literal period of time.

The basic view of Chiliasm holds that the church age is also a period of spiritual kingdom experience. However, the peace on earth that the 1000 year kingdom promised remained unfulfilled in this life, so Chiliasts looked for a future period (1000 years) of peace in kingdom with Christ. The major difference between Chiliasm and Historic Premillennialism is the emphasis that Premillennialism gives to the Jewish nature of the fulfilled kingdom, interpreting it as a fulfillment or restoration of the Jewish kingdom, this time, however, with Christ reigning as king. Chiliasm does not make as much of the restored Jewish kingdom.

It should be noted as well that Chiliasm of the early centuries was far from a unified system, but was characterized by a wide range of emphases.

## Conqueror or Conquer

A repeated theme in Revelation is *the one who conquers* or *the one who overcomes*. In each of the seven letters to the seven churches Jesus rewards those who *overcome* or *conquer*. The term is variously translated in the KJV, NIV, ASV and the NAS, RSV, NRSV Bibles. The KJV tradition and the NIV render this as *overcometh* or *overcome* while the NAS, RSV traditions render is as *conquer*. The term is a translation of the Greek noun *nikē* or the verb *nikaō*. In a war context such as Revelation the translation *conqueror* or *conquer* is preferred. In Revelation *conqueror* becomes a synonym for *martyr*, one who *conquers* Satan by dying for their faith in Jesus.

## Dispensationalism

The term "dispensationalism" derives initially from the Greek term *oikonomia* which occurs eight times in the New Testament. The term in the New Testament is translated in a variety of ways depending on the context of the term. *Oikonomia* is the root of our English word "economics" which conveys the sense of the plan, or how a something is carried on, or brought into being. The Greek term, being comprised of two words (*oikos* – house, and *nomos* – law or principle) literally means "principles by which a house operates." Of specific interest would be Eph 1:10, where the RSV translates the term as "a plan" in reference to how God would unite all things in Christ. The modern theological term, "dispensationalism," is derived from King James usage where *oikonomia* is sometimes translated as "dispensation," sometimes as "stewardship." Working out of this "dispensational" King James terminology, and with the unfortunate casting of God's saving work in terms of a time period rather than a system of operation, Dispensationalists have developed their unique doctrinal views.

In Dispensational use the term represents a period of time, differentiated from other periods of time, in which God works his plan in a specific manner. In different "dispensations" God works his plan in different ways. Each dispensation begins with an offer by God which mankind is to accept and obey, and ends with man rebelling or failing to obey God. Based on a literal interpretation of several Old Testament passages, notably Daniel 9:24-27, Dispensationalists hold that there will be seven dispensations; five before the incarnation, or first coming of Christ, one representing the church age or the age of grace, and then a final millennium or dispensation. Between the sixth and seventh dispensations there is to be a "rapture" in which believing saints will be caught up into the air to meet Christ (1 Thess 4:13-17). Toward the end of this sixth dispensation of grace, there will be an apostasy of the church which will introduce a period of tribulation (based on Dan 9:24-27). The final dispensation or the millennial kingdom will be initiated by the second coming, to earth, of Christ who will then re-establish the Jewish kingdom over which he will reign eternally. This millennial kingdom will be on earth, centered on Jerusalem, and the finalization of God's eternal plan or purpose. In this kingdom the law of God will be re-established along with the sacrificial system.

Regarding a basic view of Dispensationalist scheme we should remember, however, that Dispensationalists have through the years differed significantly in their understanding of this scheme. Each dispensation begins with an offering or promise to man by God, is followed by man's disobedience, and finally by God's judgment on man's sinful ways.

Although Dispensationalists claim that this system dates back to the early doctrines of the church, especially into the $2^{nd}$ century, Dispensationalism as we know it today dates from the early $19^{th}$ century when a new type of Premillennialism was introduced by John Nelson Darby. Darby had been educated as a lawyer, graduating from Trinity College in Dublin. Darby's academic preparation and education in the classical languages, humanities and arts was extensive and impressive. His theological education was, however, self-taught. An ordained deacon in the Church of England, Darby became dissatisfied with what he interpreted as the apathy and lethargy of the Church of England. With several others who were disenchanted with the traditional church, Darby began a "house meeting" movement which soon became known as the Plymouth Brethren; their millennial theology being designated "Darbyism." Impressed by a literal interpretation of Daniel 9, Darby divided human history into seven periods of time, or dispensations.

These periods of time, or dispensations, are listed below:
- Dispensation 1: Gen 1:28 – The period of Innocence
- Dispensation 2: Gen 3:7 – The period of Conscience and Moral Responsibility
- Dispensation 3: Gen 8:15 – The period of Human Government
- Dispensation 4: Gen 12:1 – The period of Promise
- Dispensation 6: Acts 2:1 – The period of the Church
- Dispensation 7: Rev 20:4 – The period of the Kingdom

Fundamental to Darby's Dispensationalism and those following him, was the view that the Church Age is unknown to the Old Testament prophetic system, it being "unforeseen" by Daniel and the other Old Testament prophets. This is described as the "great parenthesis" inserted between the $69^{th}$ and $70^{th}$ weeks of Daniel 9. In other words, the "kingdom clock" was stopped with the rejection of Jesus by the Jews and would only be started again at the second coming at which time the kingdom would begin.

Although Darby made several visits to the United States, beginning in 1840, where his views were adopted by Charles Henry Mackintosh and William Blackstone, "Darbyism" was "popularized" on the American theological scene primarily by Cyrus Ingerson Scofield (1843-1921), a lawyer from Kansas who became a Congregationalist minister in 1882. Early in his theological career, Scofield was influenced by Mackintosh and Blackstone, and after attending the Niagara Bible Conference where he was deeply impressed by a lecture on "Darbyism," Scofield's influence spread widely with his edition of the bible accompanied by "Notes" interpreting the Bible along Darby's Dispensational lines. So influenced was he by Darby that Scofield openly advanced the view that Darby was the most profound Bible scholar of his day. Dispensationalism in America owes much to the drive and foresight of Cyrus Ingerson Scofield who through his ministry in the Congregational Church in Dallas, his Scofield Notes in the Scofield Reference Bible, and his relationship with Lewis Sperry Chafer, minister for the Scofield Memorial church in Dallas and founder of the Dallas Theological Seminary, did much to shape American Dispensationalism along Darbyism lines. A common thread running between Darby, Scofield, and Chafer was that none of them had formal theological training.

Other significant personalities in the American Dispensational movement have been A. C. Gaebelein, Dwight L. Moody, Charles Spurgeon, Watchman Nee, John Walvoord, and Hal Lindsey.

Clarence B. Bass has defined the basic Dispensational position and view. "What, then, are the distinguishing features of dispensationalism? They are: its view of the nature and purpose of a dispensation; a rigid applied literalism in the interpretation of Scripture; a dichotomy between Israel and the church; a restricted view of the church; a Jewish concept of the kingdom; a postponement of the kingdom; a distinction between law and grace that creates a multiple basis for God's dealing with man; its view of the purpose of the great tribulation; its view of the nature of the millennial reign of Christ; its view of the eternal state, and its view of the apostate nature of Christendom." Clarence B. Bass, *Backgrounds To Dispensationalism*, (Grand Rapids: Wm. B. Eerdmans Publishing Company, 1960), p. 19.

Problems one encounters with dispensational theology are the extreme literal interpretation of Scripture, failure to see beyond a Jewish fulfillment of Scripture, extreme speculative prophetic projections (especially of Daniel 9), the restoration of the Jewish system (which amounts to a direct challenge to the all sufficiency of Christ's atoning work), and the fact that much of its theology is based on poor biblical interpretation (for example the Rapture, and the view based on Rev 20:4 ff that the kingdom would be set up on earth).

Dispensationalism is not limited to any one denominational group but cuts across such religious affiliation. There are some religious movements, however, that are significantly dispensational in orientation. These would obviously include the Plymouth Brethren, but another religious group committed to dispensationalism as a fundamental tenet of faith would be the Jehovah Witness sect. As indicated above, those graduating from the Dallas Theological Seminary would most likely be of this persuasion. It may not be an overstatement to observe that most followers of a literalist interpretation of Scripture, any biblical fundamentalism for example, would be of this persuasion. Many of the community bible fellowship churches would be dispensational in theological outlook, especially in their interpretation of Revelation.

## Eschatology

The term eschatology derives from two Greek words, *eschatos* – "last," and *logos* – "speech, word, or discussion." As a theological technical term eschatology carries the basic meaning of a "discussion of the last things or the last age." It is used in a variety of different, yet related contexts such as the second coming of Christ, the final judgment, or the final days of human history. In another "timeless" sense, the term is used in regard to "significant" events which have "end time" significance. Thus the pouring out of the Holy Spirit, repentance, baptism, and matters relating to divine activity relating to the inauguration of the kingdom are referred to as eschatological events or matters having eschatological significance. In the context of genre such as apocalyptic or Revelation, significant events such as the destruction of Jerusalem in AD 70 are often described in eschatological terminology. The intent is not to imply that such events inaugurate the final end time, but is intended to demonstrate that the event carries within it end time significance.

In the context of Revelation, the author relies heavily on both apocalyptic and eschatological genre. In one sense, much apocalyptic is eschatological in that it draws heavily on the transcendent intervention of God, and in the case of Revelation such intervention bears end time significance. Hence in Revelation much of the apocalyptic genre has eschatological implications. The use of the eschatology of Revelation is not intended to imply that the eschatological terminology describing an event is intended as a prophecy regarding some end time event. The intention is that the event being described in eschatological language simply bears end time significance.

See also Proleptic Eschatology below.

## Gnosticism

Gnosticism is a term used to designate a wide range of thought that emerged during the late 1st century AD, became a serious threat to both Judaism and Christianity in the 2nd century. The term stems from the Greek word *gnosis* meaning "knowledge." It referred to a doctrine which argued that "salvation" or "deliverance" came through the possession of a special intuitive knowledge that was possessed by those distinctively "enlightened" from above by some "deliverer" or one who would break in from "above." Gnosticism never formed a specific religion, but remained an influence or way of thinking that permeated most religions or philosophies of its day. It is not possible to define Gnosticism with any specific precision since it ranged over such a wide spectrum of thought, but a few leading concepts can be traced in most Gnostic-like communities. There was the thought derived from Platonic schools that matter was evil since matter and mankind were created by a "mischievous" or wayward child (sometimes identified with Jehovah) of the ultimate God who is absolute light and goodness. This wayward god-child also created other spirit beings which ruled the "space" between the physical world and the ultimate god of light. In order for mankind to return to this god of light they would have to negotiate space and escape these spirit beings (demi-gods) on their way back to the god of light. However, another child of this god of light, the deliverer, managed to make this journey from the god of light to mankind and enlighten certain ones, thus enabling them to return through space to the god of light by escaping the "spiritual beings in the heavenly places."

The evident similarities of this school of thought to the Christian faith made the Christian faith an obvious target for this philosophy. The challenge lay especially in the fact that this school views the physical creation as inherently evil. This would rise on Christian circles as a serious challenge to the resurrection of Jesus and eventually the general resurrection, since why would one want to raise an evil body and place a pure redeemed spirit back in captivity in the evil body? Another, even more serious challenge to the Christian faith, and one which John addressed in the Johannine Epistles, was the denial that Jesus the Christ had come in the flesh, since flesh is evil.

Other serious problems encountered in this Gnostic mindset were its obviously heretical cosmogony (an evil creation being the result of the wayward god-child, Jehovah), its challenge to God's saving activity in history (notably Jesus' death on the cross and resurrection, both seen by Christians as God's saving activity in history), and its emphasis that "deliverance" lay exclusively in possession of some special esoteric knowledge possessed by an elite community of believers. This heresy also tended to take sin lightly since sin was something intangible resulting from the flesh. Those "spiritual beings" enlightened by *gnosis* were not responsible for these sins of the flesh. This strange concept of special "grace" led to an antinomian (no law) and lascivious, licentious (one has a license to do something) attitude which was a direct contradiction to the ethical standards of both Judaism and Christianity.

Concerns over such forms of Gnostic thought (some of them Jewish forms) permeate much of the New Testament in some form, especially the Johannine Epistles. The problem in the Johannine Epistles, where John refers this mindset as the "antichrist," had to do with the denial that Jesus had come in the flesh which lay at the very heart of Christian faith. This "antichrist" flesh problem is not what we encounter in Revelation, and it would be pushing the Gnostic argument to the extreme to see Revelation as a response to this form of Gnostic thought. Since Revelation was written in the context of Ephesus and Asia Minor, which was certainly a hotbed for Gnostic thought, it is not surprising to find a possible reference to Gnostic tendencies in the references to the Nicolaitans of whom we know very little other than the fact that they appeared to be an antinomian and licentious challenge to the Christian faith. Obviously, Gnosticism and the "Antichrist" of the Johannine Epistles are not the problem addressed by John in Revelation.

## Heilsgeschichte

*Heilsgeschichte* is a German word that has become a theological technical term relating to God's plan of salvation or scheme of redemption. The fundamental theme of *Heilsgeschichte* is that God has worked his plan of salvation in the context of real history. The idea is that God's acts of salvation have taken place in real events in history according to a plan that God has been working on since the fall. This plan reached a climax in the death, burial, and resurrection of Jesus which all took place in history. Salvation is not something worked out in some form of specialized knowledge such as Gnosticism, but is located in decisive acts of God in history which are revealed as part of the process of history. *Heilsgeschichte* does not claim that history itself is salvific but that God's acts of salvation have taken place in history.

## Millennialism

Millennialism is a broad term that applies to modern interpretations of the 1000 year reign of Rev 20:4. The term derives from the Latin *mille* – "1000," and *annus* – "year." Millennial views and theories are many and different in many ways. Several sub-categories are included in Millennialism, namely, Amillennialism, Premillennialism, Postmillennialism, and Dispensationalism. Each of these is discussed in this Glossary. Basically, these theories attempt to interpret the statement in Rev 20:4 that the saints described in Rev 20:4 (martyrs) will reign with Christ for 1000 years. This millennial kingdom/reign is perceived by some to follow the Parousia or Second Coming of Jesus (Premillennialism and Dispensationalism), or to precede the Parousia or Second Coming (Postmillennialism). In either case, millennial theories have been extremely divisive in church history. One millennial view of the ancient church, Chiliasm (see the Glossary discussion of this term) was similar in some form to Premillennialism. This view in a variety of forms was most likely the dominant theory of the early church, and prevailed until Origen and then Augustine challenged the extreme literal interpretation of the biblical text upon which most millennial theories stand. In similar fashion today, Amillennial scholars challenge most millennial theories, charging that they are not the result of careful biblical exegesis and hermeneutic (interpretation), and manifest an extreme literalist interpretation of the biblical text. Other challenges to millennial theories are that they remove the message of Revelation from the 1st century church and push the message into the distant future.

## Montanism

Montanism was a late 2$^{nd}$ and early 3$^{rd}$ century heretical Christian movement originally known as the "Phrygian Heresy." In later years it was identified with, and named after its founder, Montanus (ca. AD 170). The group was characterized by ecstatic prophecy and revelations, engrossment in millennial speculation, extended periods of fasting and asceticism, and an interest in eschatologic conjecture. The movement gendered a bitter controversy with the mainline church which ultimately led to the excommunication of Montanus and the Montanist movement. Montanism's influence was significant enough, however, to sway the great church scholar Tertullian of Carthage who converted to this persuasion shortly after AD 208. Montanism gained a considerable North African following as a result of Tertullian's influence. Because of the movement's emphasis on ecstasy, revelations, and prophecy, the book of Revelation became one of the movements favored texts with the result that many mainline churches became suspicious of Revelation and resisted the inclusion of this book into the church's canon. In time, however, Revelation was looked upon in its own right and was accepted into the canon. After the 3$^{rd}$ century references to Montanism in Christian literature began to ebb with only sparse mention indicating that by the 7$^{th}$ century Montanism was no longer of any interest in church concerns.

Montanism's interest to Revelation studies is limited to references to early millennial thought, and the role this movement played in Revelation being accepted into the church's cannon. In the larger context of Christian study, the reluctance of the mainline church to accept the charismatic tendencies of Montanism indicate the declining interest and suspicion of the mainline church in charismatic expressions of Christian faith.

## Parousia

*Parousia*, like many of the terms in theological discussion derives from Greek roots. Two terms are combined producing a unique Christian technical term. *Para* – "alongside" in conjunction with *ousia* – "substance" literally means "the coming alongside in substance." In Christian dialogue the term *parousia* refers to the literal "coming of Jesus in substance," or more simply, the *second coming* of Jesus. The term is used in reference to the real, "bodily" or "physical" coming of Jesus in place of a spiritual coming as in the presence of Jesus with his church today. The term is eschatological in the sense that it refers to Jesus' coming in judgment at the end of the age.

## Postmillennialism

The roots of Postmillennialism can be identified in Christian theology as early as the century following Origen and Augustine's allegorizing hermeneutic and the church's abandonment of Chiliasm. The optimistic mindset following Constantine's "conversion" and the establishment of a universal state church paved the way for a view of the church as the arrival of the kingdom of God on earth. In the modern era, however, Postmillennialism first came into prominence in England as a result of the influence of Daniel Whitby, a Unitarian minister (1638-1726). The religious fervor and revival in America following the preaching of Jonathon Edwards and others ushered in an optimistic view of the church's potential to "convert" society and prepare it for the coming of Christ to take up his reign on earth. Postmillennialism, being an optimistic view of history and progress, thus looks toward a "golden age of spiritual growth and prosperity" as the preaching of the gospel of Christ ushers in an age religious or spiritual revival. Postmillennialists therefore interpret this period of great religious awakening and conversion as the millennial age which precedes the return and reign of Christ. The reign of Christ is thus "post-millennial." Loraine Boettner, a prominent $20^{th}$ century Postmillennialist observes regarding Postmillennialism that it is "that view of the last things which holds that the kingdom of God is now being extended in the world through the preaching of the gospel and the saving work of the Holy Spirit in the hearts of individuals, that the world eventually is to be Christianized and that the return of Christ is to occur at the close of a long period of righteousness and peace commonly called the millennium." He further observes that this period of religious awakening "is to be brought about through forces now active in the world.... The changed character of individuals will be reflected in an uplifted social, economic, political and cultural life of mankind. The world at large will enjoy a state of righteousness which up until now has been seen only in relatively small and isolated groups...it ...means that evil in all its many forms eventually will be reduced to negligible proportions, that Christian principles will be the rule, not the exception, and that Christ will return to a truly Christianized world." Loraine Boettner "Postmillennialism," *The Meaning of the Millennium: Four Views*, Ed. Robert G. Clouse, (Downers Grove: InterVarsity Press, 1977), pp.118 ff.

Alexander Campbell, and many followers of the Restoration Movement among the Disciples of Christ and Churches of Christ prior to the American Civil War were postmillennial in theological outlook. Following the trauma of the Civil War and the subsequent division of the Restoration Movement into two distinct groups, the Disciples of Christ and the Churches of Christ, Churches of Christ vacillated between a Chiliast form of Premillennialism and a tentative form of Postmillennialism.

Problems encountered with the Postmillennialist view are that Postmillennialism cannot be sustained biblically, and that it manifests an overoptimistic anthropology and an overly progressive understanding of sociology.

## Premillennialism

Premillennialism is one of those terms that can be fairly widely interpreted depending on the perspective of the interpreter! Broadly speaking the term has reference to theories of the millennium (1000 year reign of Rev 20:4) that consider the Second Coming of Christ (the Parousia) to occur immediately prior (pre) to the arrival of the millennium (from the Latin *mille* – "1000," *annus* – "year"). The impact of this doctrine is that Christ will return to earth and establish his kingdom on earth, most often located in Jerusalem. Sometimes Premillennial theories are "moderate," meaning that they simply consider the coming of the kingdom to follow Christ's Second Coming.

Views range from those that do not identify the church in any fashion with the kingdom, to those that see the church as a "spiritual" kingdom still to be fully realized on earth at some time in the future. Sometimes the view refers to a literal fulfillment *on earth*, at other times to a kingdom in heaven.

Ancient Chiliasm was premillennial in thought, and would be at one end of a continuum of premillennialism. Dispensationalism (for example, Darbyism, the Jehovah Witnesses, Scofield, Hal Lindsey, and the Dallas Theological Seminary theology) would lie at the other end of that continuum with a more fully developed dispensational theory of the millennium. (These views are discussed elsewhere in the Glossary). Toward the middle of the continuum would be the Historic Premillennialism espoused by Eldon Ladd.

A fully developed Premillennial view considers the church to be a "spiritual" kingdom with Christ reigning in the hearts of the saints from heaven, but with a fulfilled kingdom to be literally established on earth, centered in Jerusalem, with the Jewish system restored. Such views consider God's promises to the Jews to have never been completely fulfilled and yet awaiting fulfillment.

A major difference between Historic Premillennialism and Dispensationalism is the absence of a Rapture and Postponement (prophetic clock stopped) Theory in Historic Premillennialism. Both, however, stress the Jewish nature of the millennial kingdom and the fact that this kingdom will be on earth and centered in Jerusalem.

Problems encountered in Historic Premillennialism are the Jewish nature of the future kingdom, the expectation of an earthly kingdom centered in Jerusalem, the literal interpretation of the 1000 years, the view that the kingdom must be the earthly fulfillment of the promise to the Jews of an earthly kingdom over all the world, which promise was not fulfilled in the past, and the denial of the fact that the church age is really the kingdom age; that there is something lacking in the church-kingdom.

## Proleptic Eschatology

This concept derives from the word *prolepsis* which in turn derives from the Greek *prolepsis* or *prolambanein* which means to *take place beforehand, pro – before, lambano – to take*. *Eschatology* (see above under eschatology) means a discussion of end time things. In the context of eschatology proleptic eschatology means to describe, experience, or see something relating to the end time in advance of the end. The Lord's Supper or communion is a proleptic eschatological experience in the sense that during this meal the Christian experiences in advance the benefits of the great banquet eschatological banquet) that all of the saints will experience around God's table. Baptism is a proleptic eschatological experience in that in baptism one experiences in advance the resurrection to a new life in Christ. In Revelation John describes imminent judgment on Rome in terms of end of the world language. In this he is drawing on the concept of proleptic eschatological experience in that Rome is experiencing the final judgment in advance or that the judgment is expressed in advance in terms of end of the world language.

## Pseudepigrapha

The term Pseudepigrapha refers to a large group of writings falsely attributed to a person other than the one penning the work. The Greek term behind our English word simply means "false writing." In regard to New Testament Pseudepigrapha, the term refers to writings ascribed to an author other than the real writer. In the case of the Old Testament, however, the term has broader reference, namely, to literature not included in the canon, but considered sacred by early Jewish and Christian groups. Pseudepigraphy covers a wide range of literature covering what may almost be authentic to what is obviously falsely attributed to an author. Pseudepigraphy was not considered literary forger in the early years of the church since the intention of the writer was not necessarily to deceive. Early Christians considered it a matter of respect and honor to attribute their writings to one who had inspired their work. Some even argued that failure to do so was a matter of failure to honor one's predecessors. By the year

AD 120 pseudepigraphy was the norm among many Christian groups. Correctly speaking, pseudepigraphy was not the same as anonymity; pseudepigraphy was related in some fashion through a school of thought to some great person. Scholars judge only the *references* to the author to be "false," with the *content* of the writings themselves being considered invaluable for clarifying some early Jewish and Christian problems or difficulties. Some of the pseudepigraphical works were produced by learned and respected scholars. Important questions to ask pseudepigraphical writings relate not so much as to who wrote the work, but why the author wrote it and attributed it to another, and what the theme or theology of the book may be.

Examples of literature considered pseudepigraphical would be: 1 Enoch; Testament of Adam; Odes of Solomon, Apocalypse of Solomon; Apocalypse of Elijah; Ascension of Moses; 3 Corinthians; Epistle to the Laodiceans; Apocalypse of Paul; Passions of Peter and Paul; Acts of Paul; Apocalypse of Peter; Gospel of Peter; Birth of Mary; Passion of Mary; Apocalypse of the Virgin; and many others. It is obvious that some of the Pseudepigrapha are also listed among the Apocryphal books.

The reason that the Pseudepigrapha are important to Revelation studies is that much of the thought and message of Revelation is paralleled in the Pseudepigrapha, and many of the conditions of the living community were similar. Such information provides a thought and conceptual background, as well as a terminological environment, for understanding Revelation as a real living piece of literature addressed to a real living community of believers whose faith was under question and being severely challenged.

## Rebirth of Images or Recapitulation

This is a literary style in which the writer mentions a concept without developing it but will return to it in progressively as the story is developed. On each revisit to the theme it is developed in greater specificity. In the tradition of Revelation hermeneutic reaching back to the 4$^{th}$ century AD *recapitulatio*, the Latin term for recapitulation, has been explored and considered a significant literary and theological device. Austin Farrer in modern times described this device as *The Rebirth of Images*. For instance, John introduces the expression *those who dwell on earth* early in Revelation without definition or expansion. He returns to this theme and expression repeatedly adding definition and specificity to where we learn that those who dwell on earth are not all those living on earth but those who belong to the world and who worship the Roman Emperor and persecute the saints.

## Salvation

In the mindset of the apocalyptist, and Revelation is in this sense apocalyptic, salvation is not expressed in terms of individual salvation but of God's ultimate scheme of redemption (salvation) of his created universe. The apocalyptist looks beyond individual salvation to see salvation in the big picture. In this context salvation is often expressed in Revelation as *victory*, that is, the victory of God and the saints over Satan and the problem of evil and suffering. The Greek term for is *sōtēria* which according to context can be translated *healing, salvation, or victory*. Since the context of Revelation is a war between Satan and God and Satan and God's people, victory is a suitable translation for *sōtēria*. This does not mean that Revelation is not interested in the individual and individual salvation, but Revelation as apocalyptic encourages the individual to look beyond their own salvation or victory to the ultimate victory of god or of God's ultimate victory over Satan, evil, and suffering. Apocalyptic is not focused in salvation from sin but salvation or victory of God's creation over evil.

## Soon

On several occasions in Revelation John uses the word soon, for instance, Rev 1:1, where John records that God has revealed to the saints through Jesus that certain things *must soon take place*. The expression soon derives from the Greek *en tachei*.

All of our major translations (KJV, ASV, NASV, RSV, NRSV, NIV, et al) translate this as *soon* or *shortly*. Greek lexicons and grammars inform us that the adverbial phrase *en tachei* should be translated as *soon* or *shortly* and not swiftly or quickly. IN Revelation this means that eh events revealed or discussed in Revelation must soon or shortly take place. This does not mean that they will take place *quickly* when they eventually happen as futurists would have us believe.

## Time

Two Greek words are translated into English as time, *chronos* and *kairos*. *Chronos* is normally translate as time as it passes without significance. *Kairos* carries the sense of *critical, important, or significant time*. *Kairos* can be translated as crisis time. Although translated as time in Revelation the Greek word used by John is *kairos, significant time, crisis time*. The expression the time is at hand (Rev 1:3) carries the sense that *the crisis time, ho kairos eggus,* is imminent or about to break in on the readers.

## Theodicy

A theodicy is a technical term that relates to attempts to defend or explain the righteousness of an all-powerful, loving, and holy God in light of the fact of suffering and the persistence of evil. The term derives from two Greek words, *theos*, God, and *dikē, righteousness, judgment, justice*. The term carries the sense of explaining the righteousness of God in the presence of evil. One definition expresses theodicy as "A vindication of God's goodness and justice in the face of the existence of evil." Revelation is a theodicy in the sense that it attempts to explain the meaning of suffering and martyrdom by innocent people living in an evil world and facing persecution because of their faith. Revelation seeks to encourage the persecuted to see their life in the big picture of God's scheme of redemption (*Heilsgeschichte*) and to understand that martyrdom although evil is not the ultimate end of life for those who maintain faith in Jesus. The end result of suffering is fixed in the will of god and his redemptive work in the death, burial, and resurrection of Jesus. Through faith in God's working, the victory over Satan secured in the death of Jesus, and the Christian is promised victory in Jesus over Satan, death, and all suffering. Theodicy requires the individual to see life beyond the immediate present and life in the big picture of God's eternal plan or scheme of redemption.

## HCU MEDIA LLC
Publishing in support of
Heritage Christian University – Ghana (HCU Ghana)
www.hcuc.edu.gh

HCU media has been established to support the publication of materials, both paper and electronic, created by faculty and friends of HCU Ghana. These materials will be offered initially in the USA & Ghana but may become available globally via other outlets.

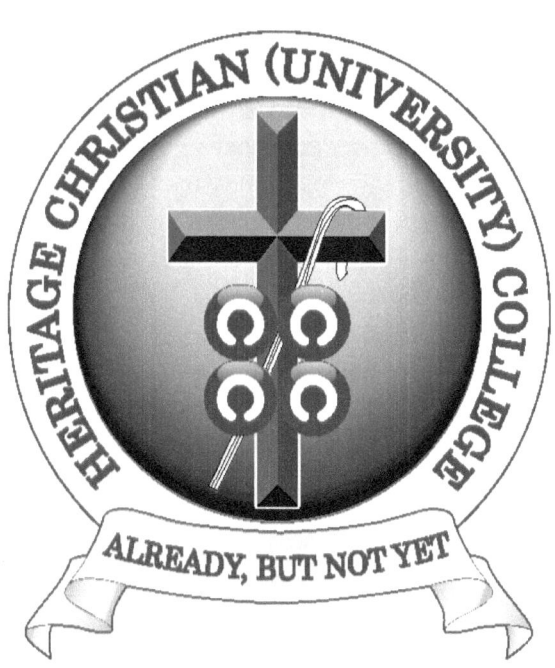

**HCU Ghana (www.hcuc.edu.gh)** is a Christian Liberal Arts University begun by the leadership of the Nsawam Rd. Church of Christ in Accra, Ghana with the assistance of many people, most notably the George Chisholm family and the faculty of Abilene Christian University. (www.acu.edu).

Commencing September 2013, HCU Ghana will offer degrees accredited by the Ghanaian national Accreditation Board (NAB) and consequently, internationally accredited bachelor degrees; in Theology, Business (Accounting, Finance, Human Resource Management, Marketing) and Information Science & Technology. HCU Ghana is affiliated with Kwame Nkrumah University of Science & Technology (www.knust.edu.gh).

**Heritage Christian College Foundation USA (HCCF USA www.hccf-usa.org)** was established in 2008 as a 501(c) 3 non-profit foundation with the purpose of providing donors the ability to provide needed seed capital and scholarship funding to the university. HCU Ghana intends to be a self-funding university but will in order to provide educations to needy students, scholarship funds are needed; most scholarship candidates will be orphans and ministry majors. Additionally, funding facilities requires the help of donors so that the costs of facilities do not become a burden to the tuition cost.

**HCU Media LLC (www.HCUMedia.com)** is the first of many entrepreneurial efforts sponsored by HCU Ghana. HCU Media is the "university press" for HCU Ghana. It will initially have offices in Plano, TX., USA and in Accra, Ghana. It will publish materials both paper and electronic which are intended to be an outlet for faculty and friends and to provide funding to the university when possible.

# Coming soon from HCU Media in early 2013!

## Kingdom Theology

This will be available in Paperback and Kindle eBook forms.
To receive notification of availability, please send an email to sales@HCUMedia.com with your request.

HCU Media LLC
P.O. Box 830
Frisco, Texas 75034

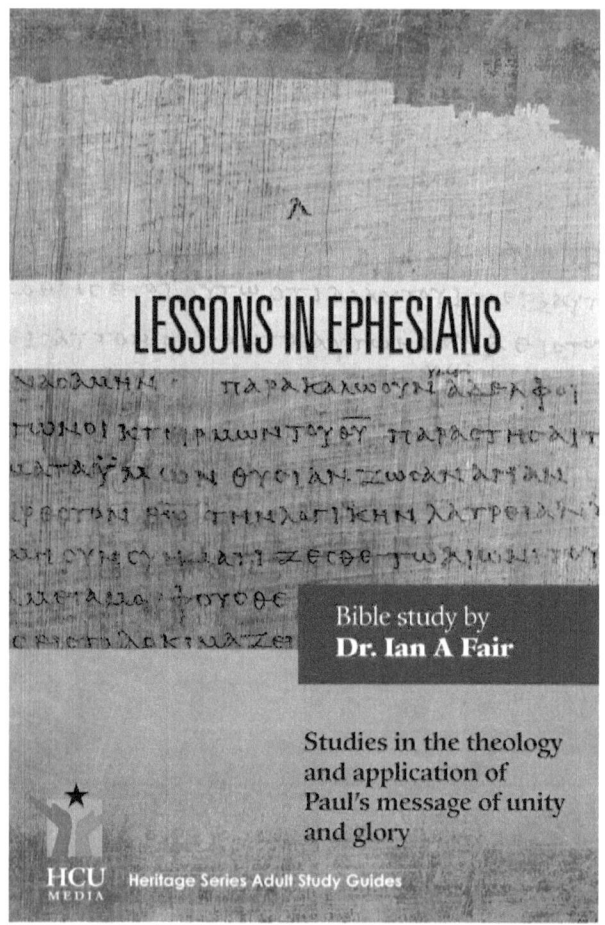

**Lessons in Ephesians**
The second in our Heritage Series Adult Study Guides, will be available in Paperback and Kindle eBook forms. To receive notification of availability, please send an email to sales@HCUMedia.com with your request.

HCU Media LLC
P.O. Box 830
Frisco, Texas 75034

# About our Author and Resources for Further Study

**Ian A. Fair (PhD)**
Professor Emeritus of New Testament
and New Testament Theology
Graduate School of Theology
College of Biblical Studies
Abilene Christian University

| TEACHING & SPECIALIZATION | SEMINARS AND WORKSHOPS |
|---|---|
| Revelation | Revelation |
| Romans | Romans |
| Prison Epistles | Matthew |
| Synoptic Gospels: Matthew | Strategic Planning |
| 1 & 2 Thessalonians | Leadership |
| Leadership | Unity in Diversity |

**Education**
Ph.D. in Systematic Theology, University of Natal, South Africa
Dissertation: *The Theology of Wolfhart Pannenberg as a Reaction to Dialectical Theology*
MA in New Testament Theology, University of Natal, South Africa
Thesis: *The Resurrection of Jesus in Three Contemporary Theologians*
BA Honors in Bible and Theology, University of Natal, South Africa
BA in Bible, Abilene Christian University, Abilene, Texas, USA
Diploma in Civil Engineering, Witswatersrand Technical College, South Africa

Dr. Fair provides further resources for study via his website at www.centercr.com. He may be contacted by going to his website and sending him correspondence.

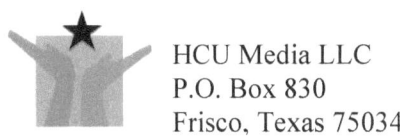

HCU Media LLC
P.O. Box 830
Frisco, Texas 75034